FREE Test Taking Tips DVD Offer

To help us better serve you, we have developed a Test Taking Tips DVD that we would like to give you for FREE. **This DVD covers world-class test taking tips that you can use to be even more successful when you are taking your test.**

All that we ask is that you email us your feedback about your study guide. Please let us know what you thought about it – whether that is good, bad or indifferent.

To get your **FREE Test Taking Tips DVD**, email freedvd@studyguideteam.com with "FREE DVD" in the subject line and the following information in the body of the email:

a. The title of your study guide.

b. Your product rating on a scale of 1-5, with 5 being the highest rating.

c. Your feedback about the study guide. What did you think of it?

d. Your full name and shipping address to send your free DVD.

If you have any questions or concerns, please don't hesitate to contact us at freedvd@studyguideteam.com.

Thanks again!

Property and Casualty Insurance License Exam Study Guide

Property Casualty Insurance Book and Practice Test Questions [3rd Edition]

TPB Publishing

Written and edited by TPB Publishing.

ISBN 13: 9781628459180
ISBN 10: 1628459182

Table of Contents

Quick Overview ---------- ***1***

Test-Taking Strategies ---------- ***2***

FREE DVD OFFER ---------- ***6***

Introduction to the Property & Casualty Exam ---------- ***7***

Types of Property Policies ---------- ***9***

Basic Insurance Principles and Definitions ---------- 9

Elements of Insurable Risk ---------- 9

Risk Management ---------- 11

Parts of the Policy ---------- 12

Property Insurance ---------- 14

Categories of Commercial Insureds ---------- 22

Flood Insurance ---------- 26

Business Owner Policies ---------- 27

Other Types of Commercial Policies ---------- 41

Types of Insurers ---------- 45

Practice Questions ---------- 58

Answer Explanations ---------- 65

Property Insurance Terms and Related Concepts ---------- ***70***

Practice Questions ---------- 84

Answer Explanations ---------- 87

Property Policy Provisions and Contract Law ---------- ***89***

Practice Questions ---------- 98

Answer Explanations ---------- 101

Types of Casualty Policies and Bonds ------------------------ ***102***

Types of Casualty Insurance -- 102

Practice Questions -- 117

Answer Explanations --- 122

Casualty Insurance Terms and Related Concepts ------------ ***125***

Casualty Insurance -- 125

Practice Questions -- 140

Answer Explanations --- 144

Casualty Policy Provisions --------------------------------------- ***147***

Practice Questions -- 153

Answer Explanations --- 155

Quick Overview

As you draw closer to taking your exam, effective preparation becomes more and more important. Thankfully, you have this study guide to help you get ready. Use this guide to help keep your studying on track and refer to it often.

This study guide contains several key sections that will help you be successful on your exam. The guide contains tips for what you should do the night before and the day of the test. Also included are test-taking tips. Knowing the right information is not always enough. Many well-prepared test takers struggle with exams. These tips will help equip you to accurately read, assess, and answer test questions.

A large part of the guide is devoted to showing you what content to expect on the exam and to helping you better understand that content. In this guide are practice test questions so that you can see how well you have grasped the content. Then, answer explanations are provided so that you can understand why you missed certain questions.

Don't try to cram the night before you take your exam. This is not a wise strategy for a few reasons. First, your retention of the information will be low. Your time would be better used by reviewing information you already know rather than trying to learn a lot of new information. Second, you will likely become stressed as you try to gain a large amount of knowledge in a short amount of time. Third, you will be depriving yourself of sleep. So be sure to go to bed at a reasonable time the night before. Being well-rested helps you focus and remain calm.

Be sure to eat a substantial breakfast the morning of the exam. If you are taking the exam in the afternoon, be sure to have a good lunch as well. Being hungry is distracting and can make it difficult to focus. You have hopefully spent lots of time preparing for the exam. Don't let an empty stomach get in the way of success!

When travelling to the testing center, leave earlier than needed. That way, you have a buffer in case you experience any delays. This will help you remain calm and will keep you from missing your appointment time at the testing center.

Be sure to pace yourself during the exam. Don't try to rush through the exam. There is no need to risk performing poorly on the exam just so you can leave the testing center early. Allow yourself to use all of the allotted time if needed.

Remain positive while taking the exam even if you feel like you are performing poorly. Thinking about the content you should have mastered will not help you perform better on the exam.

Once the exam is complete, take some time to relax. Even if you feel that you need to take the exam again, you will be well served by some down time before you begin studying again. It's often easier to convince yourself to study if you know that it will come with a reward!

Test-Taking Strategies

1. Predicting the Answer

When you feel confident in your preparation for a multiple-choice test, try predicting the answer before reading the answer choices. This is especially useful on questions that test objective factual knowledge. By predicting the answer before reading the available choices, you eliminate the possibility that you will be distracted or led astray by an incorrect answer choice. You will feel more confident in your selection if you read the question, predict the answer, and then find your prediction among the answer choices. After using this strategy, be sure to still read all of the answer choices carefully and completely. If you feel unprepared, you should not attempt to predict the answers. This would be a waste of time and an opportunity for your mind to wander in the wrong direction.

2. Reading the Whole Question

Too often, test takers scan a multiple-choice question, recognize a few familiar words, and immediately jump to the answer choices. Test authors are aware of this common impatience, and they will sometimes prey upon it. For instance, a test author might subtly turn the question into a negative, or he or she might redirect the focus of the question right at the end. The only way to avoid falling into these traps is to read the entirety of the question carefully before reading the answer choices.

3. Looking for Wrong Answers

Long and complicated multiple-choice questions can be intimidating. One way to simplify a difficult multiple-choice question is to eliminate all of the answer choices that are clearly wrong. In most sets of answers, there will be at least one selection that can be dismissed right away. If the test is administered on paper, the test taker could draw a line through it to indicate that it may be ignored; otherwise, the test taker will have to perform this operation mentally or on scratch paper. In either case, once the obviously incorrect answers have been eliminated, the remaining choices may be considered. Sometimes identifying the clearly wrong answers will give the test taker some information about the correct answer. For instance, if one of the remaining answer choices is a direct opposite of one of the eliminated answer choices, it may well be the correct answer. The opposite of obviously wrong is obviously right! Of course, this is not always the case. Some answers are obviously incorrect simply because they are irrelevant to the question being asked. Still, identifying and eliminating some incorrect answer choices is a good way to simplify a multiple-choice question.

4. Don't Overanalyze

Anxious test takers often overanalyze questions. When you are nervous, your brain will often run wild, causing you to make associations and discover clues that don't actually exist. If you feel that this may be a problem for you, do whatever you can to slow down during the test. Try taking a deep breath or counting to ten. As you read and consider the question, restrict yourself to the particular words used by the author. Avoid thought tangents about what the author *really* meant, or what he or she was *trying* to say. The only things that matter on a multiple-choice test are the words that are actually in the question. You must avoid reading too much into a multiple-choice question, or supposing that the writer meant something other than what he or she wrote.

5. No Need for Panic

It is wise to learn as many strategies as possible before taking a multiple-choice test, but it is likely that you will come across a few questions for which you simply don't know the answer. In this situation, avoid panicking. Because most multiple-choice tests include dozens of questions, the relative value of a single wrong answer is small. As much as possible, you should compartmentalize each question on a multiple-choice test. In other words, you should not allow your feelings about one question to affect your success on the others. When you find a question that you either don't understand or don't know how to answer, just take a deep breath and do your best. Read the entire question slowly and carefully. Try rephrasing the question a couple of different ways. Then, read all of the answer choices carefully. After eliminating obviously wrong answers, make a selection and move on to the next question.

6. Confusing Answer Choices

When working on a difficult multiple-choice question, there may be a tendency to focus on the answer choices that are the easiest to understand. Many people, whether consciously or not, gravitate to the answer choices that require the least concentration, knowledge, and memory. This is a mistake. When you come across an answer choice that is confusing, you should give it extra attention. A question might be confusing because you do not know the subject matter to which it refers. If this is the case, don't eliminate the answer before you have affirmatively settled on another. When you come across an answer choice of this type, set it aside as you look at the remaining choices. If you can confidently assert that one of the other choices is correct, you can leave the confusing answer aside. Otherwise, you will need to take a moment to try to better understand the confusing answer choice. Rephrasing is one way to tease out the sense of a confusing answer choice.

7. Your First Instinct

Many people struggle with multiple-choice tests because they overthink the questions. If you have studied sufficiently for the test, you should be prepared to trust your first instinct once you have carefully and completely read the question and all of the answer choices. There is a great deal of research suggesting that the mind can come to the correct conclusion very quickly once it has obtained all of the relevant information. At times, it may seem to you as if your intuition is working faster even than your reasoning mind. This may in fact be true. The knowledge you obtain while studying may be retrieved from your subconscious before you have a chance to work out the associations that support it. Verify your instinct by working out the reasons that it should be trusted.

8. Key Words

Many test takers struggle with multiple-choice questions because they have poor reading comprehension skills. Quickly reading and understanding a multiple-choice question requires a mixture of skill and experience. To help with this, try jotting down a few key words and phrases on a piece of scrap paper. Doing this concentrates the process of reading and forces the mind to weigh the relative importance of the question's parts. In selecting words and phrases to write down, the test taker thinks about the question more deeply and carefully. This is especially true for multiple-choice questions that are preceded by a long prompt.

9. Subtle Negatives

One of the oldest tricks in the multiple-choice test writer's book is to subtly reverse the meaning of a question with a word like *not* or *except*. If you are not paying attention to each word in the question, you can easily be led astray by this trick. For instance, a common question format is, "Which of the following is...?" Obviously, if the question instead is, "Which of the following is not...?," then the answer will be quite different. Even worse, the test makers are aware of the potential for this mistake and will include one answer choice that would be correct if the question were not negated or reversed. A test taker who misses the reversal will find what he or she believes to be a correct answer and will be so confident that he or she will fail to reread the question and discover the original error. The only way to avoid this is to practice a wide variety of multiple-choice questions and to pay close attention to each and every word.

10. Reading Every Answer Choice

It may seem obvious, but you should always read every one of the answer choices! Too many test takers fall into the habit of scanning the question and assuming that they understand the question because they recognize a few key words. From there, they pick the first answer choice that answers the question they believe they have read. Test takers who read all of the answer choices might discover that one of the latter answer choices is actually *more* correct. Moreover, reading all of the answer choices can remind you of facts related to the question that can help you arrive at the correct answer. Sometimes, a misstatement or incorrect detail in one of the latter answer choices will trigger your memory of the subject and will enable you to find the right answer. Failing to read all of the answer choices is like not reading all of the items on a restaurant menu: you might miss out on the perfect choice.

11. Spot the Hedges

One of the keys to success on multiple-choice tests is paying close attention to every word. This is never truer than with words like almost, most, some, and sometimes. These words are called "hedges" because they indicate that a statement is not totally true or not true in every place and time. An absolute statement will contain no hedges, but in many subjects, the answers are not always straightforward or absolute. There are always exceptions to the rules in these subjects. For this reason, you should favor those multiple-choice questions that contain hedging language. The presence of qualifying words indicates that the author is taking special care with his or her words, which is certainly important when composing the right answer. After all, there are many ways to be wrong, but there is only one way to be right! For this reason, it is wise to avoid answers that are absolute when taking a multiple-choice test. An absolute answer is one that says things are either all one way or all another. They often include words like *every*, *always*, *best*, and *never*. If you are taking a multiple-choice test in a subject that doesn't lend itself to absolute answers, be on your guard if you see any of these words.

12. Long Answers

In many subject areas, the answers are not simple. As already mentioned, the right answer often requires hedges. Another common feature of the answers to a complex or subjective question are qualifying clauses, which are groups of words that subtly modify the meaning of the sentence. If the question or answer choice describes a rule to which there are exceptions or the subject matter is complicated, ambiguous, or confusing, the correct answer will require many words in order to be expressed clearly and accurately. In essence, you should not be deterred by answer choices that seem excessively long. Oftentimes, the author of the text will not be able to write the correct answer without offering some qualifications and modifications. Your job is to read the answer choices thoroughly and completely and to select the one that most accurately and precisely answers the question.

13. Restating to Understand

Sometimes, a question on a multiple-choice test is difficult not because of what it asks but because of how it is written. If this is the case, restate the question or answer choice in different words. This process serves a couple of important purposes. First, it forces you to concentrate on the core of the question. In order to rephrase the question accurately, you have to understand it well. Rephrasing the question will concentrate your mind on the key words and ideas. Second, it will present the information to your mind in a fresh way. This process may trigger your memory and render some useful scrap of information picked up while studying.

14. True Statements

Sometimes an answer choice will be true in itself, but it does not answer the question. This is one of the main reasons why it is essential to read the question carefully and completely before proceeding to the answer choices. Too often, test takers skip ahead to the answer choices and look for true statements. Having found one of these, they are content to select it without reference to the question above. Obviously, this provides an easy way for test makers to play tricks. The savvy test taker will always read the entire question before turning to the answer choices. Then, having settled on a correct answer choice, he or she will refer to the original question and ensure that the selected answer is relevant. The mistake of choosing a correct-but-irrelevant answer choice is especially common on questions related to specific pieces of objective knowledge. A prepared test taker will have a wealth of factual knowledge at his or her disposal, and should not be careless in its application.

15. No Patterns

One of the more dangerous ideas that circulates about multiple-choice tests is that the correct answers tend to fall into patterns. These erroneous ideas range from a belief that B and C are the most common right answers, to the idea that an unprepared test-taker should answer "A-B-A-C-A-D-A-B-A." It cannot be emphasized enough that pattern-seeking of this type is exactly the WRONG way to approach a multiple-choice test. To begin with, it is highly unlikely that the test maker will plot the correct answers according to some predetermined pattern. The questions are scrambled and delivered in a random order. Furthermore, even if the test maker was following a pattern in the assignation of correct answers, there is no reason why the test taker would know which pattern he or she was using. Any attempt to discern a pattern in the answer choices is a waste of time and a distraction from the real work of taking the test. A test taker would be much better served by extra preparation before the test than by reliance on a pattern in the answers.

FREE DVD OFFER

Don't forget that doing well on your exam includes both understanding the test content and understanding how to use what you know to do well on the test. We offer a completely FREE Test Taking Tips DVD that covers world class test taking tips that you can use to be even more successful when you are taking your test.

All that we ask is that you email us your feedback about your study guide. To get your **FREE Test Taking Tips DVD**, email freedvd@studyguideteam.com with "FREE DVD" in the subject line and the following information in the body of the email:

- The title of your study guide.
- Your product rating on a scale of 1-5, with 5 being the highest rating.
- Your feedback about the study guide. What did you think of it?
- Your full name and shipping address to send your free DVD.

Introduction to the Property & Casualty Exam

Function of the Test

Individuals seeking employment as property and casualty insurance agents must typically pursue and obtain licensing from the state in which they wish to be employed. State examination procedures vary based on the requirements of each individual state, but states typically require that candidates for a license pass an exam on property and casualty insurance as part of the licensing process.

Because property and casualty insurance exams are part of states' insurance agent licensing processes, the typical test-taker is a young adult wishing to begin a career as a property and casualty insurance agent, or an adult wishing to switch careers into the field of property and casualty insurance. Sometimes, insurance agents licensed in other fields of insurance will take the exam in order to get licensed for property and casualty.

Test Administration

Details of where, when, and how often property and casualty insurance exams are administered vary from state-to-state. Some states use in-house testing procedures, while many outsource their examinations to third-party testing centers. For instance, Alaska, Arkansas, Colorado, Delaware, Georgia, Hawaii, Illinois, Iowa, Kansas, Maine, Missouri, Nevada, North Carolina, Rhode Island, Tennessee, Texas, Virginia, West Virginia, and Wyoming offer property and casualty insurance examinations through Pearson VUE, while Arizona, Connecticut, Massachusetts, Nebraska, New Hampshire, New York, Ohio, South Dakota, Vermont, and Wisconsin offer exams through Prometric. States typically do permit retesting for test-takers who do not pass a property and casualty insurance exam on their first attempt, although some states do place limits on retesting. For example, some states may only permit a limited number of retest attempts or require that test-takers wait a certain amount of time before attempting the test again.

All states are required to make accommodations for test-takers with disabilities in keeping with the Americans with Disabilities Act. This typically means that a test-taker with a documented disability can receive accommodations such as additional time or specialized printed material for an exam. Test-takers requiring accommodations should contact potential employers prior to registering for the exam.

Test Format

The format of a property and casualty insurance exam varies from state to state, but the tests are generally considered quite challenging, and typically go into detail about policies, rules, and regulations related to property and casualty insurance. A typical state might ask around 100 multiple-choice questions covering every aspect of insurance policies and sales, including types of policies, policy riders, policy exclusions, insurance policy applications, tax and retirement implications of insurance policies, as well as state-specific laws and regulations pertinent to the sale of such policies.

Scoring

Scoring methods and requirements also vary from state to state, with most states calculating a raw score based on the number of correct answers given with no penalty for incorrect answers or guesses, and then converting that raw score to a scaled score with a set minimum passing score.

Recent/Future Developments

States are regularly changing the details of the test they require, so interested applicants should check with their state for the latest information about changes.

Types of Property Policies

Basic Insurance Principles and Definitions

Insurance dates back to 1750 BCE when Chinese and Babylonian traders divided their wares among several different ships so that they would not lose all of their goods should one of their ships sink or be taken over by a hostile party. Known as the **transference of risk**, insurance still follows those basic principles today. **Insurance companies** provide loss coverage for many clients, knowing that every insured will not incur a loss, dividing the company's risk to cover the losses of a few that is paid for by many.

Risk is the probability that a loss will occur by way of injury, natural disaster, negligence or any negative occurrence. **Pure risk**—also known as **absolute risk**—is the possibility that a loss will occur that results in a loss to the insured and is the only type of loss that can be insured. Examples of pure risk include fire, theft, and injury. Any pure risk loss will have a negative effect on the insured. **Speculative risk** holds the possibility of gain and is not insurable. Examples of speculative risk include investing in the stock market and gambling. Since the outcome of a speculative risk is unknown, these types of risks cannot be insured.

An insurance company's **underwriting department** uses various criteria to determine the risk exposure for each type of policy they sell. For example, they may determine that hurricanes or earthquakes are known to occur in a certain geographical area and thus limit or exclude coverage for those weather events in order to avoid having to pay for catastrophic losses. In addition, insurance companies may require that specific preemptive actions be taken by an insured before offering coverage. For example, if an inspection showed that the stairs leading to an insured's place of business were in disrepair, they may require the stairs be repaired before offering coverage.

An **insured** is defined as the owner(s) of a property insurance policy. Additional insureds covered under a property policy include members of the insured's family residing with them, those less than 21 years of age in the care of any insured on the policy—excluding losses to those persons incurred while the insured is engaging in a business, such as a day care, unless specifically covered under the insurance policy—up to two boarders or roomers, and one additional family.

Elements of Insurable Risk

Not all types of losses can be insured. In order to determine if a loss can be insured, the insurance company uses the following criteria:

- Losses must be predictable—i.e., with enough frequency and average severity—so that it allows insurers to establish a premium. For example, an insurance company could look at statistical data that details the amount of losses incurred as the result of a certain peril, such as a hurricane, before deciding to provide coverage and determining what premium to charge.

- Insurance companies have to protect themselves against adverse selection by having enough measures in place to accurately decide whether to offer coverage and determine what premium to charge. Adverse selection occurs when one party withholds information that would influence the other party's actions. For example, on an auto policy an insured may give his or her insurance company a different address because he/she lives in an area where comprehensive premiums—those for fire, theft, glass, and vandalism—are higher due to increases instances of vehicle theft. In order to combat this practice, an insurance company may ask for a piece of mail from a service provider, such as a cable company, as proof of residence.

- The loss must be fortuitous or unexpected. An example would be a fire that occurs as the result of an electrical outlet the insured did not know was faulty is an unexpected loss.
- Losses must be measurable and definable. For example, if a structure is lost due to a fire the insurance company can calculate the amount of coverage to offer because they know the cost to rebuild. However, if a third party reported an injury after falling down a flight of stairs—but cannot produce any evidence of the injuries—the insurance company could not determine how much to reimburse them.
- Losses cannot be catastrophic in nature. For example, if a storm completely destroyed all structures over a large geographical area, an insurance company may not have the reserve funds to cover all of the losses.
- Loss exposures must be randomly selected. This means that insurers cannot use adverse selection in setting premiums. Adverse selection means that insurers must avoid concentrating their business in risk categories by classifying them according to age, occupation, economic statues, or geographical area. This action protects members in the same class from being adversely affected by insureds who make frequent claims or claims in high dollar amounts.
- Losses must be random in nature and must be applied using the law of large numbers. Random losses are not predictable, such as a fire caused by a faulty outlet that the insured was not aware of. Using the law of large numbers, the insurance company spreads their risk exposure over a large geographical area. For example, the insurance company will determine what premium to charge on their property policies based on how many losses are expected to occur within a certain city's limits.

A **hazard** is any element that increases the possibility of a loss. For example, if an insured regularly leaves his/her house unlocked when not at home, the possibility increases that he/she may incur a loss due to theft. A **morale hazard** occurs when an insured unconsciously changes behavior and doing so leads to an increase in the probability a claim will occur. For example, if an insured who is tired of looking at her dreary office is not as careful as she should be about keeping things neat and tidy, it increases the possibility that someone could trip over the mess.

A **moral hazard** constitutes an insured's conscious change in behavior that could lead to a loss, such as a snowboarder who performs increasingly difficult tricks because he knows he has medical insurance. A **physical hazard** is an instance that could lead to a claim, such as a set of stairs the insured knows is rotting but does not repair or replace, thus leading to the possibility that a third party could be injured.

A **peril** is any occurrence that is covered or excluded under an insurance policy. For example, a fire, which is an **insured peril**, may be covered whereas damage caused by the deliberate action of an insured, an **excluded peril**, would not be covered.

Insurers **indemnify**—financially compensate for harm or loss—when they pay an insurance claim. In order for a claim to be paid, there must be an insurable interest. For example, an insured may have a car replaced if it is stolen; however, someone borrowing an insured's car at the time it was stolen would not be able to receive a car as the borrower suffered no financial loss from the theft. A good statement to remember in regard to **indemnity** is "You cannot insure something you do not own or have a financial interest in."

Risk Management

Risk management is a formalized process for dealing with the inherent uncertainly of risks. The risk management process includes identifying, assessing, and prioritizing risks. There are five ways to manage risks:

- **Avoid risks**: Insurance companies do not insure risks that are known to cause losses beyond what they are able or willing to insure.
- **Retain** or **self-insure risks**: An individual or company may have enough assets to not need insurance because he or she can afford to pay for any losses. One exception to this is when it is required by law to obtain insurance, such as liability insurance for a vehicle to cover third party damage.
- **Control risks** by preventing or reducing them: Insurance companies will mitigate their losses by making sure measures are in place that prevent claims or, at least, reduce the likelihood of a claim. For example, requiring that a structure have smoke and fire detectors installed as a condition of the insurance policy is a way to prevent risk.
- **Transfer** or **insure risks**: Individuals or businesses that cannot afford to pay for any insurable losses they may incur will purchase an insurance policy, thus transferring the duty to pay for a loss from themselves to the insurance company.
- **Share risks**: If a risk is insurable but potential claims could cause the insurance company to incur huge financial losses, two or more insurance companies may insure the same risk and share in any payment of claims.

The **Insurance Services Office** (ISO), a subsidiary of Verisk Analytics, is the advisory and rating organization for the property and casualty insurance industry in the United States. The ISO provides insurance companies with actuarial, statistical claims, underwriting, and other information they can use to determine their policy wordings and the premiums they charge. Each insurance company's policies will vary depending on how they interpret the information provided by the ISO, and individual states have their own insurance statutes.

Parts of the Policy

Policy Declarations

The **policy declarations** section details the type of coverage, location, and time frame and includes the following:

- The named parties—who is covered
- The type of property—structures and property
- Eligible insured location(s)
- Policy period
- Coverage limits
- Deductibles—amount payable by the insured toward any losses that occur

Insuring Agreement

The **insuring agreement** states the major promises of the insured, lists the risks that the insurer assumes under the contract, and includes a reference to the contractual agreement between the insurer and the insured.

Conditions and Exclusions

The **conditions** detail the shared rights and responsibilities of the insurer and the insured. Common conditions include the following:

- **Liberalization**: Policy provision that increases coverage without additional premium. For example, if an insurance company decides to start covering all claims resulting from windstorm damage, all eligible policies already in force will automatically receive this coverage, but the insurance company cannot charge any additional premium to the insured for the coverage.

- **Assignment clause:** A condition that disallows the insured from transferring benefits to another party without the insurance company's permission. For example, if an insured has water damage to his home, he cannot hire a company to clean up the damage and tell that company to send the bill to the insurance company. This can only be done if the insured reports the water damage claim and if the insurance company agrees to pay the cleanup company for their work to repair the damage.

- **Subrogation:** The legal right for the insurer to recoup their financial losses from a third party. For example, an insured is in a car accident, and her insurance company initially pays for the damage. If the accident is proven to be the fault of a third party, the insurance company can recoup their financial losses from the third party.

- **Appraisal:** Allows the insured to request an appraisal when the amount of loss is disputed. Both the insured and the insurance company will acquire individual appraisers. They usually agree to accept a blended amount as calculated by the appraisers. Appraisal clauses differ between policies.

- **Duties after a loss:** A provision that details duties required of the insured after a loss. Some examples include notifying insurer or preventing further damage.

- **Mortgage clause:** Requires the lender to meet the terms of the agreement if the insured does not pay premiums

- **Other insurance clause:** Details how the insurers settle claims when there is more than one insurance company. These clauses are included so they can comply with the principle of indemnity that states an insured cannot benefit financially from a loss. For example, an insured purchases two insurance policies to cover the same property, each insuring the house for $100,000. If the house is destroyed by a fire, the insured cannot collect $100,000 from both insurance policies to pay for the loss as this would total $200,000, an obvious financial gain for the insured.

- **Loss settlement:** Requires the property to be insured for at least 80% of the replacement cost as a co-insurance condition, in order for the insurer to reimburse the insured for replacement cost to the dwelling and other structures.

The **exclusions** eliminate coverage for specific perils on all policies. In some, but not all cases, the insured may be able to purchase coverage for an excluded peril either for an additional premium or on a separate policy. Examples include, but are not limited to, the following:

- Earthquake and earth movement
- Flooding and water overflow
- War or acts of terrorism—whether or not war is declared
- Riots, demonstrations, or civil commotions
- Nuclear reaction, radiation, or radioactive contamination
- Building addition, repair, or demolition due to new laws or ordinances
- Power outages if the source of loss is located off the premises
- Government seizure or demolition of property
- Intentional acts by the insured
- Negligence or damage caused by the insured's failure to take appropriate action after a loss

Coverage Limits

There are three ways for insurers to cover property:

- **Specific:** Provides coverage for a single item with a specified limit
- **Scheduled:** Provides coverage for multiple items and sets different limits for each item
- **Blanket**: Provides coverage for multiple items under one policy with a total, or aggregate, limit

Perils and Losses

Perils refer to the cause of the loss and are classified as named perils and open perils:

- **Named peril** policies state that if a peril is not specifically listed, the peril is not insured.
- **Open peril**—or **all-risk** coverage policies—state that if a peril is not specifically excluded then it is covered.

Loss refers to physical damage to property, bodily injury, loss of use, or loss of income. There are two types of losses: direct loss and indirect loss.

- **Direct loss** is damage to real property or personal property that was caused by a covered peril.
- **Indirect loss** is a loss that occurs as a result of a direct loss. Examples of indirect loss include loss of income and increased expense to live or conduct business at another location.

Loss Valuation

The **loss valuation clause** details how a loss will be calculated. There are four methods to value a loss:

- **Actual cash value:** Replacement cost of the item less depreciation
- **Replacement value:** Repair or replacement of the item at current retail or market cost
- **Stated or agreed value:** Replacement at agreed amount, regardless of appreciation or depreciation
- **Valued policy:** Provides the amount stated in the declarations for covered items that are a total loss

Coinsurance refers to the amount the insured must pay for a loss. A deductible is a common type of coinsurance.

Property Insurance

Property insurance is a policy that financially reimburses the owner or renter of a structure for a covered loss to the structure or other property. Homeowner's policies and commercial package policies have two sections.

Section I: The Property Section

Coverage A: Dwelling Coverage

This coverage includes the dwelling and any structures that are attached to it. Examples of attached structures include an attached porch, an awning, an attached garage, etc. Coverage A also includes fixtures and systems that service the dwelling such as plumbing, electrical wiring, heating, and permanently-installed air conditioners.

Coverage B: Other Structures

This includes **detached structures** that are located on the premises. Other structures include swimming pools, sheds, fences, barns, guest cottages, etc. Coverage B is limited to 10% of the limit of Coverage A.

Coverage C: Personal Property

This coverage includes contents in the home that are not attached to the home. Personal property is nearly everything that can be picked up and carried out. It also covers personal property of the insured's guests and employees—as long as the employee is not engaged in an activity relating to a business of the insured—in any residence that the insured occupies. Coverage C will also cover the personal property of others if their property and the insured's property are located in the same area of the insured's residence.

Personal property is covered anywhere in the world, with some limitations. Property that is stored away from the insured's residence is limited to 10% of Coverage C or $1000, whichever is greater. If the insured's residence is being repaired or is uninhabitable, the personal property is covered in a temporary residence of the insured. Personal property is covered for up to thirty days when an insured moves to a new principle residence.

Coverage D: Loss of Use

This pays for reasonable housing and living expenses that the homeowner incurs as a result of a covered loss, while the dwelling is being repaired or rebuilt. This includes hotel or rental fees, dining out, extra mileage, etc. It is important to note that loss of use provides coverage over and above normal living expenses. For example, if it is expected that an insured would spend $200 per week for groceries, the insurance company would take that amount into account when calculating reimbursement of expenses for meals. In calculating the allowable amount, the insurance company would consider that the cost of eating meals at a hotel, as opposed to the insured's own home, is considerably higher and would adjust the allotment for meals accordingly.

Section II is the casualty section and is discussed in a later section.

Homeowner's Property Forms

Dwellings that are eligible for homeowner policies must be used exclusively as a residence. Some policies include **incidental occupancies**, such as a temporary residence at a private school or an in-home office or studio.

Dwellings must have four or fewer family units to be eligible. Dwellings may also be eligible if they are under construction, used as a seasonal or secondary residence, homes being paid off under installment contracts, homes that are occupied under trusts or estates, or are mobile homes when the mobile home endorsement has been added.

Farms are not eligible for homeowner's policies.

There are seven different personal property policies for homeowner's insurance. These forms include policy forms for unit/condominium owners, renters, and landlords. They are HO1, HO2, HO3, HO4, HO5, HO6, and HO8.

The **HO1 Basic Form** is known as a **named-perils-only policy**. Only coverage for the dwelling is included unless the policy specifically extends coverage to the personal property or contents. Perils that are covered are fire, lightning, smoke, hail, windstorm, vehicles (including aircraft), riot/civil unrest, volcanic eruption, malicious mischief, vandalism, explosion, and glass breakage. The acronym W.C. Shaver is often used to help remember perils covered on the basic form (windstorm, civil commotion, smoke, hail, aircraft, vehicles, explosion, and riot). Excluded perils include floods and earthquake damage. Most insurance companies no longer offer this form of insurance coverage.

The **HO2 Broad Form** (ISO HO 00 02) is a named perils policy that covers the dwelling, personal property, and liability. If a peril is not specifically named, then it is not covered. Coverage on this policy form extends to the following:

- Weight of ice, sleet or snow, unless it damages fences, patios, awnings, pavement, swimming pools, piers, bulkheads, docks, or similar structures
- Falling objects—must damage the exterior of the dwelling first
- Freezing of plumbing or water systems—unless dwelling is vacant, and insured has not taken precautions to prevent freezing
- Sudden and accidental overflow from water or steam systems
- Vehicle damage to fences, driveways, and walkways—even when caused by a vehicle that is owned or operated by a resident of the insured property
- Smoke damage from fireplaces

The **HO3 Special Form** (ISO HO 00 03) is the most comprehensive coverage form available to an insured. It is known as an **all perils policy**: unless a peril is specifically excluded, it is covered. Personal property is covered on a named perils basis, meaning coverage is limited to only those perils that are listed. An all perils named policy is misleading in nature. It is important to remember that all insurance policies have exclusions, and not every known peril can be insured. The HO3 policy lists the following specific exclusions:

- Collapse, unless it is included under other coverages
- Theft relative to a building that is under construction
- Vandalism and malicious mischief (V&MM) when a building has been vacant for more than 60 days
- Freezing of plumbing, heating, or similar systems when the building is under construction, unoccupied, or vacant, unless the insured took precautions to protect it
- Water or ice damage—freezing, thawing, weight, and pressure—to fences, patios, or pavements
- Damage by animals or insects that are owned by the insured
- Cracking, shrinking, expanding, and bulging of pavements, foundations, walls, and similar surfaces
- Natural wear and tear, rust, corrosion, agricultural smudging, and other gradual, expected losses
- Emission of smoke, vapor, chemicals, fumes, waste, and similar pollutants

Some of these perils can be **endorsed**—added on—to the policy for an additional premium.

The **HO4 Contents Broad Form (**ISO HO 00 04) is for tenants who lease or rent a dwelling. This is a named perils policy that covers the tenant's personal property and liability for unintentional acts of the insured. If a peril is not specifically listed, coverage is excluded.

The **HO5 Comprehensive Form** (ISO HO 00 05) is for tenants who lease or rent a dwelling. This is an all perils policy that covers the tenant's personal property and liability for unintentional acts of the insured. If a peril is not specifically excluded, it is covered.

The **HO6 Condominium Unit Owner's Form** (ISO HO 00 06) is designed for owners of condominiums and cooperative units. This form covers the condominium or cooperative homeowner's portion of responsibility for the unit, including improvements and betterments. It includes coverage for the tenant's personal property in addition to liability for unintentional acts of the insured. It is a named perils policy. If a peril is not specifically named, coverage is excluded.

The **HO8 Modified Coverage Form** (ISO HO 00 08) is a named-perils-only policy that is used to insure an owner-occupied dwelling where the cost to replace the dwelling in the event of a loss would far exceed the property's current value. An example would be a dwelling that meets the necessary codes but was built using substandard or cheap materials and is destroyed by fire. The insurance company would replace the dwelling, but it reserves the right to acquire used building materials and build a replacement structure that is very basic in nature. This type of policy prevents insureds from benefitting due to a loss, meaning they would not, for example, be able to install hardwood flooring and crown moldings at the expense of the insurance company when rebuilding a very basic home.

Mobile homes can be insured by a stand-alone mobile home package policy, which is a specialized form that is designed to cover mobile homes and manufactured homes. Coverage is similar to a homeowner's policy, including property, loss of use, and liability. Mobile homes can also be insured by adding an endorsement to an HO2, HO3, or dwelling form. There are specific requirements when coverage for a mobile home is offered. For example, the mobile home must be tied down.

Endorsements

An **endorsement** is a change that is made to a policy that adds, modifies, or excludes coverage. Coverage that is not included in policy forms or is excluded can be added back into the policy, usually with an additional premium. Endorsements can be added to include coverage for earthquake damage to personal property, home day care coverage, water back up coverage, refrigeration spoilage, identity theft, and permitted incidental occupancy such as a home office.

Personal Inland Marine Property Forms

Inland marine coverage policies cover losses to specialized property. Inland marine coverage evolved as a result of ocean marine insurance policies that provided coverage for cargo that was in transit in addition to the vessels used in the transport of goods. Though inland marine coverages are not "marine" in nature, the insurance industry has never developed another, perhaps more appropriate, name for this type of policy.

Inland marine coverage can be stand-alone policies or added as an endorsement to an existing policy. Six categories constitute types of inland marine coverage that is offered: personal property floaters, commercial property floaters, domestic shipping, imports/exports, and instrumentalities of transportation and communication, including bridges and towers. Those purchasing inland marine coverage include contractors, professional musicians, medical professionals, companies transporting cargo, museums, computer businesses, professional photographers and warehouse owners. Property that is regularly in transit or in the custody of a bailee for which coverage is available includes construction equipment, movie production equipment, professional musical instruments, medical equipment, solar panels, and fine arts.

Coverage is provided on a named peril or all perils basis. The inland marine policy will state the method by which the value of the insured property will be calculated. The calculation methods used are the following:

- **Actual cash value:** The replacement cost of the property minus depreciation
- **Market value:** The value of the property if sold as used, which comprises value determinations such as the condition of the property at the time of the loss and the demand for the property in a resale market
- **Repair value:** The cost to repair the property to restore it to the original condition of the property before the loss
- **Replacement value:** The cost to replace the property that was lost with property as close as possible to the property that was lost

On a homeowner's property policy, some additional coverages are reflected as percentages of the value of the insured dwelling. These additional coverages are other structures on the property, personal property, and loss of use—living expenses over and above normal living expenses incurred as the result of a loss. Personal liability and medical payment limitations are determined by the insurance company. Even if the property insurance policy reflects the coverage as a blanket limit—meaning coverage for the dwelling, other structures, personal property, and loss of use—the insurance company can still limit the maximum amount of coverage for the additional coverages. For example, if a fire were to destroy a house and a detached garage, the insurance company would limit the amount of the claim settlement that can be used to rebuild the garage. This is to prevent the insured by benefitting from a loss—for example, building a garage with a second story finished living space when the garage lost was a single story.

Coverages A (dwelling), B (other structures), C (personal property), D (loss of use), E (personal liability), and F (medical payments) have different limits based upon the policy type.

This chart shows how these limits are determined:

Coverages	HO-2	HO-3	HO-5	HO-8
A-Dwelling	primary limit determined by insured	primary limit determined by insured	primary limit determined by insured	primary limit determined by insured
B-Other structures	1–2 family dwellings = 10%	1–2 family dwellings = 10%	1–2 family dwellings = 10%	1–2 family dwellings = 10%
	3–4 family dwellings = 5%	3–4 family dwellings = 5%	3–4 family dwellings = 5%	3–4 family dwellings = 5%
C-Personal property	1–2 family dwellings = 50%	1–2 family dwellings = 50%	1–2 family dwellings = 50%	1–2 family dwellings = 50%
	3 family dwellings = 30%	3 family dwellings = 30%	3 family dwellings = 30%	3 family dwellings = 30%
	4 family dwellings = 25%	4 family dwellings = 25%	4 family dwellings = 25%	4 family dwellings = 25%
D-Loss of use	30% of Coverage A	30% of Coverage A	30% of Coverage A	10% of Coverage A
E-Personal liability	$100,000	$100,000	$100,000	$100,000
F-Medical payments	$1,000	$1,000	$1,000	$1,000

Coverages	HO-4	HO-6
A-Dwelling	None	None
B-Other structures	None	None
C-Personal property	determined by insured	determined by insured
D-Loss of use	30% of Coverage C	50% of Coverage C
E-Personal liability	$100,000	$100,000
F-Medical payments	$1,000	$1,000

The limits shown in the table are minimum limits, which may be increased.

Dwelling Property Forms

Dwelling policies—also known as **dwelling fire policies**—provide coverage for some types of dwellings that cannot be covered by a homeowner policy. Dwelling forms can be stand-alone policies, or they can be added to a homeowner policy.

Dwelling policies are appropriate for landlords who own tenant-occupied one, two, three, or four-family dwellings. Homeowners who don't qualify for a standard homeowner policy, due to past claims, poor property conditions, or other reason, can get a dwelling fire policy for an owner-occupied dwelling. Dwelling policies can also be written for mobile homes at a fixed location, vacant dwellings, and personal property that is contained in eligible dwellings.

Dwelling policies are not standard policies in that they are provided for special situations and may contain exclusions, parameters, and requirements on the part of the insured that are not normally part of an insurance policy. For example, if the insureds have an unacceptable amount of past claims, they may have a very high deductible, as much as $10,000. If a dwelling is vacant, the insured may be required to check the property on a daily or weekly basis in order for coverage to stay in place.

Loss Settlement and Insurance to Value

Personal property for dwelling policies is settled on an actual cash value basis. Insureds can purchase replacement cost insurance for an additional premium, but the policy will only provide coverage if the loss is from a named peril.

Most homeowner and dwelling policies require that the dwelling be insured to 80% of its replacement cost. Dwellings that are not **insured to value**—80% of replacement costs—may be subject to a coinsurance clause. If the policy limit for the dwelling doesn't meet or exceed 80% of the replacement cost, the insurer only pays the greater of depreciated cost or actual cash value.

Dwellings that are not insured to 80% will be settled according to the **coinsurance formula**:

$$insurance\ carried \div the\ insurance\ required\ \times the\ amount\ of\ the\ loss$$
$$= amount\ of\ payment\ by\ the\ insurer$$

The insured is still liable for the policy deductible. Here's an example:

Replacement cost: $600,000

$$\$600{,}000 \times 80\% = \$480{,}000$$

$$\frac{Amount\ Carried}{Amount\ Required} = \frac{\$400{,}000}{\$480{,}000} = 0.833\ coinsurance\ penalty$$

Loss scenario:

$$0.833\ penalty \times \$80{,}000\ loss - \$1{,}000\ deductible = \$65{,}667$$

$$Insurance\ pays\ \$65{,}667$$

$$Insured\ pays\ \$13{,}333 + \$1{,}000\ deductible$$

Additional Coverages

Homeowner policies include coverages for specific things at no additional premium for the insured. Here are some additional coverages:

- **Debris removal**: This additional coverage covers costs of removing debris from damage caused by a covered peril.
- **Tree debris removal**: The policy will pay up to $1000 per occurrence and up to $500 per tree under certain circumstances. Tree and tree debris removal applies when a tree damages a covered structure, the tree blocks the entrance to a driveway or designated thoroughfare, or the tree blocks a handicapped-accessible entrance or feature. The tree must have fallen due to

wind, hail, or weight of ice or snow. Tree debris coverage will also pay for removing a neighbor's tree that falls due to any peril that is covered under Coverage C.

- **Trees, shrubs, and other plants**: This coverage pays up to $500 per tree, shrub or plant, if they are damaged or lost due to fire, explosion, lightning, riot, theft, V&MM, or aircraft not owned or operated by an insured. Most HO-2, HO-3 and HO-5 policies apply a limit of 5% of the Coverage A limit. HO-4 and HO-6 policies limit coverage to 10% of the Coverage C limit or $500 per tree, shrub, or plant.

- **Reasonable repairs**: This coverage applies to extra costs that an insured incurs when trying to prevent further loss. Examples include costs to board up windows or tarp a roof. Insureds are required, as stated in the insurance policy, to take any reasonable action required in order to prevent further loss from occurring.

- **Property removed**: Covers property as it is being moved from a location that has the potential to damage it from a covered peril. Coverage is limited to 30 days.

- **Loss assessment:** This coverage covers losses that are assessed to an insured by a homeowner or property association where there is a direct, covered loss to common property of members of the association. The maximum payment is $1000 per occurrence.

- **Fire department service charge**: The coverage pays up to $500 for the cost of a fire department call to save the property from a covered peril. This payment is not subject to the deductible and cannot be paid unless the homeowner incurs out-of-pocket expenses.

- **Credit card, electronic fund transfer card, or access device, forgery, and counterfeit money**: This coverage pays the insured up to $500 for lost or stolen credit cards or forged checks. It also pays for expenses when an insured unknowingly accepts counterfeit money. The coverage does not cover the insured's business activities or dishonesty, and payments are not subject to the deductible. Also, this coverage only takes effect if the insured's expenses are not otherwise waived or reimbursed. For example, if the bank waives the replacement cost for a credit card, the insured cannot recoup the usual replacement cost for the credit card since the insured did not actually incur that cost.

- **Collapse**: This coverage pays for loss due to building collapse that results from a covered or additional named peril. Coverage is not offered on HO-8 policies.

- **Landlord's furnishings**: This coverage pays for personal property, appliances, carpeting and other household items that belong to the insured and are used by a tenant of the insured. The coverage is available on HO-2, HO-3, and HO-5 policies and is limited to $2500 per loss.

- **Grave markers**: This coverage pays for losses to grave markers and mausoleums up to $5000 for perils that are named under Coverage C. Applicable policy forms are HO-2, HO-3, HO-4, HO-5 and HO-6.

- **Glass or safety glazing material**: This coverage pays for losses to doors, windows, and skylights, such as broken glass.

- **Building additions and alterations**: This coverage is available for HO-4 policies to pay for losses to building alterations, additions, and improvements that the insured paid for. The coverage is limited to a maximum of 10% of Coverage C.

- **Ordinance or law coverage**: This coverage pays for repairs to structures that need to be updated to meet current building codes, ordinances, or land use codes. It is available on HO-2, HO-3, HO-4, HO-5, and HO-6 policies with a maximum limit of 10% of Coverage A.

Categories of Commercial Insureds

Commercial and business owner policies are classified under the following types of businesses:

- **Individual or sole proprietorship:** Includes named insured and his or her spouse
- **Partnership or joint venture:** Includes named insured, any partners or members, and managers
- **Limited liability company (LLC):** Includes named insured members and managers
- **Other organizational structures:** Corporations, cooperatives, and S-corporations

An insured who is a spouse, partner, member, or manager is only covered while he or she is performing job functions as part of the insured's business. The coverage also extends to the insured's employees.

Commercial Property Insurance

Commercial property insurance covers property that is owned, operated, or controlled by a business. There are different forms included in commercial property insurance packages. They include the following:

- Commercial property cause of loss provides coverage for one of the property forms—basic, broad, or special.

- Building and personal property coverage provides coverage for building damage caused by direct loss, damage to business personal property, and damage to personal property of others.

- Builder's risk coverage provides coverage for damage to buildings and structures that are under construction. This also includes foundations, fixtures, equipment, and materials used in construction.

- An earthquake and volcanic eruption endorsement can be added as an endorsement to a commercial property form for loss due to earthquake or volcanic eruption for an additional premium.

- A spoilage endorsement is available on the building and property coverage forms and condominium commercial unit-owners coverage forms. It covers perishable stock that is subject to spoiling when not kept in a controlled environment.

- A value reporting endorsement is coverage for property that has regular changes in value, such as seasonal retail products. It also applies to property that is moved between locations. The insured reports the actual value of property on a value reporting form. The insurer uses the data to calculate the insurance amounts and premiums.

- Ordinance or law coverage endorsement is coverage that pays the increased costs that are required to repair or rebuild after a covered loss to comply with current building ordinances or laws.

Commercial property insurance covers the following against damage from insured perils:

- Permanent buildings and structures owned by the business
- Additions, fixtures, equipment, and machinery permanently installed
- Outdoor fixtures (stand alone signs may require additional endorsements) and furniture
- Fire extinguishers, removable floor coverings, and appliances (microwave, refrigerator)
- Repairs and additions to the permanent buildings and structures (unless they are covered under another insurance policy, such as a builder's risk)
- Temporary structures, supplies, and equipment that are within 328 feet of the permanent buildings and structures
- Items held or maintained for the purpose of adding to or altering the building and structures
- Contents used in the operation of the business located within the premises or within 328 feet of the premises
- Property that is in the care, custody, and control of the business
- Tenants betterments and improvements defined as additions, alterations, fixtures, and installations (if performed by the insured at their own expense and if the insured does not own the building or structure)
- Stock being held for sale by the business
- Accounts receivables that cannot be collected due to the destruction of records and the reasonable costs associated with restoring the records
- Bailee customer goods (property of a customer that is in the temporary possession of the business)

Losses that pertain to the following are excluded from coverage. Policy endorsements or additional insurance policies may be available that will provide coverage for these losses.

- Money, bank notes, currency of any kind, lottery tickets, securities
- Invoices and bills
- Animals (unless held as stock or boarded for a fee)
- Damage to any land or paved surfaces
- Damage to boilers, machinery, buildings, or any structures if their foundations are below the lowest basement floor or, if there is no basement, the surface of the ground)
- Water damage (except as the result of extinguishing a fire, optional coverage available)
- Inventory shortages where there is no evidence to indicate a theft
- Laws or ordinances
- Retaining walls (if not part of a permanent structure)

- Electronic data
- Any underground equipment (drains, pipes)
- While any property is waterborne or airborne
- Signs (unless attached to a building)
- Fences, flowers, trees, shrubs (unless considered stock)

Commercial Property Forms

Commercial property forms include the basic, broad, and special forms, similar to the personal property forms. The **Commercial Property Basic Form** (ISO CP 10 10) provides coverage for named perils including the following:

- Fire
- Lightning
- Explosion
- Smoke
- Windstorm
- Hail
- Riot and civil commotion
- Aircraft
- Vehicles
- Vandalism
- Sprinkler leakage
- Sinkhole collapse
- Volcanic action

The **Commercial Property Broad Form** (ISO CP 10 20) provides coverage for the named perils covered on the basic form, plus the following:

- Falling objects
- Weight of ice, snow, or sleet
- Water damage
- Collapse from a specified cause

The **Commercial Property Special Form** (ISO CP 10 30) provides open peril or all-risk coverage for perils, unless they are specifically excluded.

Commercial Package Policy Forms

A commercial policy that combines different coverages under one package is called a **Commercial Package Policy** (CPP). The commercial package policy consists of two parts: the declarations page and the conditions page.

The **common policy declarations** page provides basic pertinent information about the policy, including the named insured and mailing address, the policy period, a description of the business, and a list of coverages purchased that includes endorsements, premium amounts, and types of necessary forms.

The **common policy conditions** page details the duties and responsibilities of the **first named insured** on the policy. The named insured is responsible for premium payments, making policy changes, cancelling policies, book and record examinations/audits, inspections and surveys, notifying the insurer of loss, and the transfer of rights and duties.

In addition to the declarations and conditions, the commercial package policy also includes two or more of the following coverages:

- Buildings and personal property
- Business auto
- Commercial general liability
- Commercial crime
- Commercial inland marine
- Farm
- Employment practices liability
- Professional liability
- Boiler and machinery
- Personal and advertising injury liability

Commercial Inland Marine Insurance

Commercial inland marine policies cover losses for commercial property—goods and products—that is transported over land and is not at a fixed location. Commercial property covered under this form is covered on an open perils basis. Property must meet the following criteria to be eligible for commercial inland marine property policies:

- Must be in transit
- Must be moveable
- Must be related to transportation of communication
- Must be in possession of a bailee

The nationwide commercial inland marine definition includes six types of insurance property:

- Imported goods and merchandise
- Exported goods and merchandise
- Domestic shipments and property for sale or consignment while in transit
- Bridges, tunnels, and communication towers
- Property not usually held at a residence
- Property related to a business practice or profession

Commercial inland marine property is classified as filed or non-filed:

Filed inland marine classes—Commercial inland marine items that are uniform and common are called filed classes because the classes can be standardized, and the rating information can be calculated. These are also called **floaters**. Filed classes include the following:

- Accounts receivable
- Camera and musical instrument dealers
- Floor plan merchandise
- Implement dealers
- Jewelry dealers

- Musical instruments
- Negative film
- Photo equipment
- Physicians' and dentists' equipment
- Signs
- Theatrical property

Non-filed inland marine classes—Items that are classified as non-filed inland marine property items are too diverse or too subject to change to be classified in groups or to be accurately rated as a class. Non-filed classes include items such as cargo, construction, electronic data processing, farm, and other diverse risks.

Flood Insurance

Flood insurance covers buildings and personal property against losses from flooding due to inland or tidal water overflow, mudslides, rapid water runoff or accumulation, erosion, or land collapse that is caused by flooding. Damage caused by water below the ground's surface that leaks or seeps into the dwelling is excluded.

National Flood Insurance Program (NFIP)

The NFIP is a flood insurance program that is funded by the federal government to aid communities that are affected by flooding. The flood insurance program is administered by the Federal Emergency Management Agency (FEMA), a subsidiary of the U.S. Department of Homeland Security.

In order to be covered under the NFIP, the community where the residence or commercial property is located must be a participant in either the regular or emergency flood insurance program. Emergency coverage begins as soon as a community applies for coverage; however, coverage is limited to $35,000 for buildings and $10,000 for building contents during the application process.

Once the application process is completed and approved, and rates are established, the community is admitted into the regular program. The regular flood insurance program insures buildings up to a maximum of $250,000 and building contents to a maximum of $100,000.

Buildings are always covered at replacement cost as long as they are insured to 80% of the market value or at the maximum allowable level of coverage. Buildings that are not insured to value will be covered on an actual cash value basis. Building contents are always covered on an actual cash value basis.

Flood insurance covers the building, its foundation, equipment, and systems used to service the building. It also covers refrigerators, stoves, and built-in dishwashers. Flood insurance will cover permanently installed carpeting over unfinished flooring, window blinds, and permanently installed paneling, wallboard, and built-ins such as bookcases and cabinets.

Detached garages can be covered up to 10% of the building property, but other detached buildings require a separate policy. Building contents that are covered under flood insurance differ slightly from homeowner policies. Flood insurance will cover everything that can be picked up and carried out. Contents also include washing machines and dryers, food freezers and food spoilage, and certain valuable items, such as fine arts and furs with a $2500 limit for each of those classes of items.

Business Owner Policies

Commercial property, commercial liability, and commercial package policies are available for most types of businesses that are well established. However, these policies may be unaffordable for a small to medium-sized business, so another form of commercial insurance—the business owner policy—was developed for smaller or less established businesses.

A **Business owner policy** (BOP) is an insurance property and liability package for certain types of businesses that need a specific type of coverage and operate out of a single location. The BOP was developed when the Insurance Services Office (ISO) ascertained that certain types of businesses could not afford the premiums charged for commercial policy packages of insurance and did not require such broad and extensive coverage; the businesses also held less risk than larger, more established, companies.

BOP policies have restrictions pertaining to the number of employees, the annual amount of gross income, and the type of property where the business is located. BOP policies do not include professional liability, commercial or personal auto insurance, workers' compensation, health insurance, or disability insurance. However, BOP policy owners can purchase supplemental coverages as needed. Depending on their industry and the specifics of their business, they may be required by law to purchase coverage such as workers' compensation.

In addition, if the business is a franchise of a large recognized chain, they may not be eligible for a BOP policy, even though they technically may meet the individual business requirements. This is due to the fact that a national chain, for example, is subject to increased claims merely as the result of the perception by the public that they will pay claims as opposed to potential exposure to negative publicity.

Requirements for the issuance of a BOP policy vary between insurance companies and states. Eligibility for a BOP policy is determined by considering the class of business, location of the business, size of the business in regard to employees, and annual gross revenue. Thus, the following parameters should be regarded as a general representation only and may not apply to all BOP policies. Businesses insured under a BOP policy may include the following:

- **Auto**: Body shops, glass shops, muffler and brake repair shops
- **Food:** Deli, fast food, fine dining, pizza, small independent restaurant
- **Retail:** Clothing, electronics, furniture, books, appliances, wholesalers
- **Service:** Barber shops, beauty salons, tanning salons, dry cleaners, funeral homes, pet grooming

Certain types of small businesses are not eligible for BOP policies:

- Manufacturers
- Auto repair or service stations
- Vehicle dealers—autos, motor-homes, mobile homes, and motorcycles
- Parking lots and parking garages
- Bars, pubs, and cocktail lounges
- Amusement parks and attractions
- Banks and financial institutions
- Self-storage facilities that provide outdoor storage of motorized vehicles
- Certain contractors
- Household property

- One and two-family dwellings
- Certain wholesalers

BOP Occupancy and Size Restrictions

The following outlines risks that may be written on a BOP policy. It should be reiterated that BOP policy requirements vary between insurance companies and between states. Thus, the following is a general representation of the general provisions needed for a BOP policy to be issued.

Buildings

Apartments, residential condominiums, and residential condominium associations of any size may be insured on a BOP. Occupancy may include offices, mercantile, processing, eligible wholesalers, and service. Commercial unit-owners and office buildings may not be over six stories high and cannot be over 100,000 square feet in the size of their geographical footprint (GFP). Other buildings may not exceed a total of 35,000 square feet in size (GFP). Occupancy for these types of buildings must be principally mercantile, eligible service and processing operations, or contractors.

Business Personal Property

Business personal property can be covered in any office with less than 35,000 square feet (GFP). For mercantile operations, wholesale, or eligible service and processing operations they should not exceed 35,000 square feet (GFP) and $6 million in annual gross sales. Business personal property may be insured at any insured location.

Service and processing businesses have an additional restriction that no more than 25% of annual gross sales may be realized from off-premises operations. For example, if a small restaurant offers catering services and their annual gross revenue is $1,000,000, no more than $250,000 of that annual gross revenue can be earned from catering.

Contractors

Certain types of contractors including residential carpenters, residential drywall contractors, painters, and landscape contractors may be insured under a BOP. Coverage is limited to contractors in buildings with less than 35,000 square feet (GFP) per location, with no work being performed at a height of over three stories. The contractor business may not have more than $300,000 in annual payroll.

Restaurants

Restaurants, including fast food restaurants that prepare or serve cold food or food that is cooked using small appliances that don't emit smoke or grease-laden vapors may be eligible for a BOP. The restaurant premises is limited to less than 7,500 square feet (GFP) and must have a seating capacity of 75 patrons or less and a sign from an inspecting official, such as a fire marshal, must be posted. A seating capacity of up to 150 patrons may be accommodated under a BOP policy if certain conditions are met. The restaurant may serve alcohol when it is limited to beer or wine and sales of alcoholic beverages are less than 25% of the total annual gross sales. A restaurant where the sale of alcoholic beverages exceeds 25% of the total annual gross sales, though classified as a restaurant, would be ineligible for coverage.

Convenience Stores with Gasoline Pumps

Convenience stores with gasoline pumps may be insured under a BOP form provided that gasoline sales don't exceed 75% of the total annual store sales. These locations may not provide automotive service or repair, operate car washes, or offer propane or kerosene tank filling.

Laundries and Dry Cleaners

Laundries and dry-cleaning businesses may be insured under a BOP when the insured location is less than 35,000 square feet (GFP). The business must have fewer than three pick-up locations, and the annual gross sales must be less than $6 million.

Wholesalers

Wholesalers must also meet the 35,000 square feet size (GFP) limit, with no more than 25% of the total square footage being open to the public. Wholesalers must also have annual gross sales below $6 million, with no more than 25% of sales from retail operations.

Motels

Motels are eligible for a BOP when they are less than three stories high and do not have a bar or cocktail lounge on the premises. Seasonal establishments must not be closed for more than 30 consecutive days annually.

Self-Storage Facilities

Coverage is limited to buildings that have less than three stories. Cold storage and industrial waste storage facilities are not eligible.

Perils Covered

Due to the limited risk in comparison with commercial forms, most BOP policies provide open peril coverage and are written on the special form. Some BOP policies can be endorsed to named peril coverage with the following covered perils for an additional premium:

- Lightning
- Fire
- Windstorm and hail
- Smoke
- Explosion
- Vandalism
- Riots and civil commotion
- Aircraft and other vehicles
- Volcanic eruption, excluding the cost to remove ash or other particles that did not cause damage to an insured premises or property
- Leaking fire extinguishers and their equipment
- Sinkholes
- Water damage
- Weight of ice, sleet, and snow
- Falling objects

The following losses are not covered regardless of whether they were caused by other causes or events:

- Civil authority
- Earth movement
- Fungus or related perils
- Nuclear hazard
- Ordinance or law

- Utility failure
- War and military action—whether or not war is declared
- Water
- Weather—when connected to the losses excluded above

Additional Exclusions

The BOP also excludes the following causes of loss:

- Animals
- Collapse—except as provided under additional coverages
- Computer virus or hacking
- Contamination or deterioration
- Criminal, fraudulent, dishonest, or illegal acts
- Defects, errors, or omissions
- Electrical currents
- Explosion
- Freezing
- Mechanical breakdown
- Neglect
- Pollutants
- Seepage
- Settling, cracking, shrinking, bulging, or expanding
- Smog
- Smoke, vapor, or gas
- Temperature or humidity
- Virus or bacteria
- Voluntary parting of title or possession because of fraudulent scheme, trick, or false pretense
- Wear and tear

BOP Coverage Limitations

The BOP has the following specific limits regarding the amount or type of coverage for a covered loss:

- Boilers and steam equipment are not covered when the loss is due to equipment failure. The BOP will cover a loss that is caused by gas or fuel explosion that occurs inside the firebox, combustion chamber, or flue or within the flues or passages through which the gases of combustion pass.

- Furs, fur garments, or garments trimmed with fur have a limit of $2,500 for any one occurrence for loss by theft.

- The policy excludes breakage of fragile articles such as glassware, statuary, porcelains, and bric-a-brac, except as a result of perils that are specified in the policy. This exclusion does not include glass that is part of a building or structure, bottles or containers that are being held for sale, or lenses of photographic or scientific instruments.

- The interior of the building or structure damage is not covered if the loss is due to rain, snow, sleet, ice, sand, or dust—even if it is driven by wind—unless the rain, snow, sleet, ice, sand, or dust entered through an opening that was created by a covered peril, or the loss or damages were caused by thawing of snow, sleet, or ice in the building or structure.

- Jewelry, watches, watch movements, jewels, pearls, precious or semi-precious stones, or metals—e.g., gold, silver, platinum bullion—have a coverage limit of $2,500 total in any one occurrence for loss by theft when the jewelry or watches are valued at $100 or more.

- Animals are not covered unless damage is caused by an insured peril and then only if they are deceased or their death is made necessary.

- Fragile items, such as china, marble, and porcelain, are not covered if broken, unless the items were part of the interior or exterior building, scientific or photographic lenses, or containers that were being held for sale.

- Missing property is not covered when the cause of loss is mysterious disappearance, a shortage is discovered during inventory, or any instance where there is no physical evidence that would explain the loss of the property.

- Patterns, dyes, molds, models, or forms are covered with a limit of $2,500 total in any one occurrence for loss by theft.

- Personal property is not covered for damage caused by rain, snow, ice, or sleet when left out in the open.

- Loss or damage to property that has been transferred to a person or to a place outside the described premises on the basis of unauthorized instructions is not covered.

The BOP covers buildings, business personal property, loss of income, and liability that is covered by a named peril.

Section I: Property coverage

Coverage A: Building coverage

Coverage A covers all buildings and parts of buildings up to the limit shown on the declarations page. It includes the following:

- Buildings and structures located on the premises

- Completed additions

- Machinery and equipment that are permanently part of the described building or structure

- Fixtures including outdoor fixtures

- Personal property of the insured that is used to maintain or service the property, including air conditioning equipment, fire extinguishers, outdoor furniture, floor coverings, and appliances

- Additions under construction, alterations, and repairs to the building or structure

- Materials, equipment, supplies, and temporary structures that are on or within 100 feet of the described premises when used for making additions, alterations, or repairs, if not covered by other insurance

- Personal property of the insured as a landlord furnished in apartments, rooms, or common areas

Coverage B: Business Personal Property

Business personal property is covered in the buildings and structures that are described on the declaration page. It is also covered when it is out in the open, in vehicles, or when located within 100 feet of the described premises, up to the limit shown on the declarations. Business personal property includes the following:

- Property of the insured that is used in the business

- Property of others that is in the care, custody, and control of the insured, plus cost of the insured's labor, material, and services, unless otherwise provided for in the Loss Payment Property Loss Condition

- Personal property leased by the insured where there is a duty contractual obligation to insure the property, unless the property is insured elsewhere

- Improvements made to a building or structure where the insured is a tenant—including fixtures, alterations, installations, or additions, including building glass—and when the improvements were made at the insured's expense and cannot be legally removed

Business Personal Property That is not Covered

Certain types of property are not covered under Coverage A or Coverage B. Some types of coverages can be added back in on a limited basis under **Additional Coverage or Extended Coverage** or by an endorsement for an additional premium. As previously stated, there are certain perils that are always excluded and for which no type of insurance can be purchased. Property not covered includes the following:

- Accounts receivables
- Signs that are not attached to buildings, fences, or antennas-including masts, towers, and satellite dishes
- Contraband or illegally transported property
- Shrubs, plants, and trees—unless they are part of additional coverages—hay, grain, or other crops that are outdoors
- Land, water, or crops
- Lottery tickets that are not held for sale
- Money, securities, accounts, bills, or food stamps
- Valuable papers and records are not covered for the cost to reproduce, replace, or restore
- Vehicles, aircraft, or self-propelled machines that are required to be licensed for use on public roads, including permanently-installed computers in vehicles
- Watercraft and their motors, equipment, or accessories while in the water

Additional Coverages

Most BOP policies are written on a special form and automatically include additional coverages with no additional premium. Coverage limits are on a per-occurrence basis. The following additional coverages outline general coverages, exclusions, time limits, and coverage amounts and percentages, with further provisions and limitations in specific policy wordings:

Debris Removal

When the cause of loss is a covered peril, the policy will pay 25% of the sum of the deductible plus the stated amount for direct physical damage or loss. If the maximum limit on debris removal is insufficient to reimburse the cost of debris removal, the insurer will pay up to an additional $10,000 only if the actual expense exceeds the limit of insurance and if the actual expense exceeds the 25% of the sum of the deductible plus the stated amount for direct physical damage or loss. This expense must be reported within 180 days of the date of the damage. Coverage does not apply to extraction of any type of pollutants to remove, restore, or replace any polluted land or water. For example, the limit of the insurance is $90,000. The deductible is $500. The amount of the loss is $80,000. This means the loss payable amount is $79,500 ($80,000 minus the deductible of $500). The expense for debris removal is $30,000. The coverage amount available for debris removal is calculated as follows: $80,000 ($79,500 + $500) X 25% =$20,000. But it's capped at $10,500. The cap of $10,500 applies because the amount of the loss payable ($79,500) and the basic amount for the debris removal expense ($10,500) cannot exceed the limit of insurance ($90,000).

Preservation of Property

The policy covers property for up to 30 days as it is being moved or stored, when the insured moves it to another location to protect it from loss.

Fire Department Service Charge

The policy pays up to $2500—unless a different limit is stated in the declarations—when the fire department is called upon to save or protect covered property, and the insured is contractually or legally obligated to pay the fee.

Collapse

The policy covers loss that occurs when a building cannot be inhabited because all or part of it has fallen down—unless the BOP is endorsed with the named perils coverage. Perils insured for collapse include vermin or insect damage—unless the insured was aware of the damage or decay—use of defective materials if the abrupt collapse occurs during construction, renovation, or remodeling. Collapse after construction, renovation, or remodeling can be covered, but only if the collapse is due to vermin, decay, a specified cause of loss, glass breakage, weight of rain that collects on a roof, or weight of persons or personal property. There is limited coverage for items other than the building, such as walkways, awnings, retaining walls, etc.

Water Damage, Other Liquids, Powder or Molten Material Damage

The policy covers the building when water, liquids, powder, or molten material indirectly escapes and also covers repair of replacement of the system that is responsible for the escape if the building is covered by other insurance.

Business Income

The policy reimburses the insured for business income that is lost if the business must close due to a covered loss. Coverage applies if the business closes due to direct physical damage to business property that is located on or within 100 feet of the insured premises or if in the open or in a vehicle, and the damage resulted from a covered peril. Coverage continues for 12 months following the day of the loss and is paid independently of the limits that are set in the policy. The coverage includes ordinary payroll for up to 60 days, unless a different time frame is stated in the declarations. Ordinary payroll includes wages, employee benefits directly related to payroll, FICA payments made by the insured, union dues, and workers compensation premiums.

- The coverage is subject to a 72-hour deductible, which means the business owner pays the initial expenses for the first 72 hours after the loss. Business income is not subject to coinsurance.
- Depending upon the circumstances surrounding the loss, the policy may offer extended business income coverage, which will continue making payments even once the business has been restored, until the business meets the pre-loss earnings threshold or until some other condition in the declarations has been met. The coverage continues for up to 30 days with the option to increase the number of days.
- Extra expense: This covers extra expenses that occur because of damage to the property described on the declarations. Coverage is limited to within 12 months after the date of loss, and the 72-hour deductible does not apply.
- Pollutant clean up and removal: This coverage pays up to $10,000 aggregate per policy period.
- Civil authority: This coverage extends business income and extra expense coverage if a civil authority prevents the insured from accessing the premises described on the declarations, due to direct physical loss or damage to the property by a covered cause of loss. Coverage also extends to a covered cause of loss other than at the described premises, but not more than one mile from the described premises. Business income coverage begins 72 hours after the civil action and continues for up to four consecutive weeks. Extra expense coverage begins immediately after the civil action.
- Money orders and counterfeit money: This coverage reimburses the insured for accepting counterfeit currency and/or money orders in exchange for goods and services up to $1000.
- Forgery and alteration: This coverage applies when the insured suffers loss because checks, drafts, promissory notes, or other documents have been forged. The coverage includes reasonable legal expenses with a limit of $2500 or the limit that is stated on the declarations pages.
- Increased cost of construction: This coverage applies when there are extra costs because a building must be rebuilt to current ordinances or codes. The coverage only applies to buildings that are covered for replacement cost and have a limit of $10,000, unless otherwise stated in the declarations.

- Business income from dependent properties: A dependent property is one that delivers the insured's materials or services, accepts the insured's products or services, or manufactures goods that will be delivered to the insured's customers. The dependent property does not need to be scheduled on the policy, but it must be located in the coverage territory as stated on the policy and must attract the insured's customers to the insured's business. This coverage extends business income coverage to losses that damage dependent properties and begins 72 hours after the covered loss or damage occurs. The limit is $5000, and higher limits may be purchased.

- Glass expenses: This coverage pays for glass that is part of the building, temporary plates, and for boarding up openings temporarily. This coverage does not extend to cover window displays.

- Fire extinguisher systems recharge expense: This coverage pays up to $5000, per occurrence, to recharge or replace fire extinguishers and systems, whichever is less. It also covers property that is damaged from accidental discharge of fire extinguishers, unless such damage occurs during testing or installation.

- Electronic data: This covers the cost to replace or restore damage to electronic data that is lost or damaged due to a covered loss, with a limit of up to $10,000. It covers loss due to computer viruses or other such harmful code as long as they are not due to manipulation by an employee of the insured. Higher limits may be purchased.

- Interruption of computer operations: This coverage pays for damage to computers and computer systems as a result of a covered loss and is limited to a maximum of $10,000 unless higher limits are stated in the declarations or purchased as additional coverage.

- Limited coverage for fungi, wet rot, dry rot and bacteria: This coverage reimburses for costs to remove the presence, growth, proliferation, or spread of fungi, wet rot, or dry rot due to a covered loss and is subject to a limit of $15,000.

Coverage Extensions

In addition to the property coverages in Section I of the BOP, coverage can be extended to the following property when it is in or on a building that is described on the declarations, is out in the open or in a vehicle, and is within 100 feet of a building that is described on the declarations. Coverage extensions have a separate limit of liability and include the following:

Newly Acquired or Constructed Property

This extension covers up to $250,000 for newly-acquired buildings and up to $100,000 for personal property that is moved to a newly-acquired building or premise, when the building or property is acquired during the policy term. Coverage lasts for up to 30 days of the acquisition of the property or 30 days from the time construction begins, unless the policy expires prior to that time. The extension also expires when the insured reports actual values to the insurer. Reported values higher than the limits stated on the policy may be subject to an additional premium.

Business Personal Property off Premises

This extension covers business personal property up to $10,000 while it is in transit or is temporarily stored at another location that is not owned, leased, or operated by the insured. Property excluded from coverage include money, securities, and valuable papers and records.

Outdoor Property

This extension covers perils of fire, lightning, aircraft, riot, and explosion—known as the FLARE perils—with a limit of $1000 per tree, shrub or plant, and a maximum of $2500 total. It also covers other outdoor property, such as fences, signs, and radio or television antennas. These totals include coverage for debris removal expenses.

Personal Effects

This extension covers up to $2500 for business personal property coverage at each premise that is described on the declarations for personal effects that are owned by the insured and the insured's employees. Coverage does not include tools and equipment used in the insured's business nor loss of any personal effects by theft.

Valuable Papers and Records

This extension pays for the costs to research, replace, or restore information on lost or damaged valuable papers and records for which there are no duplicates. It limits coverage for up to $10,000 on the premises and up to $5000 off premises.

Accounts Receivable

This extension covers payments that the insured is unable to collect due to damage to the insured's accounts receivable records and includes additional coverage for interest expenses, collection expenses and other reasonable expenses to reestablish the accounts receivable records. It also reimburses for costs to collect outstanding payments up to $10,000 on premises and up to $5000 off premises.

Section II: Liability Coverage

Under Section II of the BOP, the insurer agrees to pay for damages that the insured is legally required to pay because of bodily injury, damage to property, or personal and advertising injury for which the insurance applies. The insured has the right to investigate and settle claims.

Premises and Operations

Liability also covers liability exposure that occurs from the **premises or operations** of the business. The occurrence must occur inside the territory specified in the policy and during the policy period.

Products and Completed Operations

The BOP will cover product liability exposures that relate to **products**, goods, and merchandise of the business that is manufactured, sold, handled, distributed, or disposed of by the business. Liability includes coverage for **completed operations,** which are losses that occur after the work is completed, and the insured has left the worksite. The policy offers contingent liability for the actions of others who are under the control of the insured, including individuals who are working for the insured on a contractual basis.

Personal and Advertising Injury Liability

The liability portion of the BOP includes **personal and advertising injury liability**. The insured must be legally liable for personal or advertising injuries for the coverage to be claimed. If there is no harm to another party, there is no coverage. Personal or advertising injuries include the following types of offenses:

- Malicious prosecution
- False arrest or imprisonment
- Using the advertising ideas of another person
- Infringing upon the copyright, trade, or slogan of another business
- Oral or written slander towards another person or organization
- Violating another person's right to privacy
- Degrading goods or service of another person organization
- Wrongful eviction
- Wrongful entering
- Violating a person's right of private occupancy
- Consequential bodily injury

Medical payments

Section II of the BOP also includes medial payments per person, with a limit of $5000. **Medical payments** are made whether the insured is at fault or not, in order to prevent more expensive lawsuits. Typical expenses may include ambulance fees, emergency room fees, hospital costs, costs for x-rays, dental costs, funeral costs, and aid that is rendered at the site of an accident. Injuries must have occurred on or adjacent to the insured premises or due to the insured's business operations. The injury must occur within the coverage territory while the policy was effective, and it must be reported within a year of the occurrence. Medical payments do not cover the insured, the insured's employees, injuries that occur on residences that the insured owns or rents as an occupancy, or people who are covered by workers' compensation.

Supplementary Payments

Payments may be made on a supplementary basis in addition to the standard policy limits, meaning supplementary payments do not reduce the limit of liability. **Supplementary payments** may be made for the following:

- Defense and legal expenses incurred by the insurer in defending a claim or lawsuit
- Cost of bail bonds related to bodily injury on vehicles, with a $250 limit
- Cost of bonds to release attachments
- Reasonable expenses incurred by the insured to aid in investigating or defending a claim or lawsuit, including up to $250 per day for lost earnings for time off work
- Court costs that the insured is required to pay because of a lawsuit
- Prejudgment interest the insured is required to pay
- Interest that accrues after a judgment is made and before it is paid

BOP Liability Exclusions

Certain bodily injury and property damage are excluded from the BOP policy. They include the following:

- Injuries that arise out of expected or intentional injury

- Those in the business of manufacturing, distributing, selling, serving, or furnishing alcoholic beverages

- Work-related injuries that are covered under workers' compensation or employer's liability laws
- Pollution losses that result in bodily injury, property damage, or clean-up costs
- Losses that result from the maintenance, operation, or use of aircraft, autos, or watercraft, except as specified in the policy
- Acts of war—whether or not war is declared—and terrorism
- Damaged to the insured's work that arises out of the insured's product
- Loss that arises out of the transportation of mobile equipment by auto, use of mobile equipment in racing or related activities, or while practicing for racing activities
- Failure to provide any professional services
- Liability assumed under a contract or agreement
- Claims based on defects, deficiencies, inadequacies, or dangerous conditions in the insured's products or work, and delays or failures to perform contracts properly
- Product recalls as a result of known or suspected defects
- Damage to impaired property or property that has not been physically damaged
- Electronic data as the result of the loss of use of the data due to corruption or the inability to access or manipulate the data
- Criminal acts
- Recording or distributing any information that is prohibited by law
- Medical expenses for any insured—except volunteer workers—for a person hired to do work on behalf of an insured or an insured's tenant or for any person who usually occupies the part of the premises the insured owns or rents, if expenses are covered under any other policy or benefit
- Body injury or damage caused by any nuclear event, unless otherwise provided for in the declarations

BOP liability also lists specific exclusions related to personal and advertising injury losses, including the following:

- Oral or written statements or publications that the insured knows to be false
- Criminal actions of the insured
- Breach of contract
- Liability assumed under a contract—unless insured has liability without a formal contract
- Failure of goods or services to meet quality standards
- Incorrect advertising of products or services
- Offenses that an insured commits during the business of advertising, publishing, broadcasting, or telecasting

Optional Coverages

BOP policies typically include coverages that are available as options by endorsement for an additional premium. Optional coverages include the following:

Outdoor Signs

This option covers direct physical damage or loss to all outdoor signs that are owned by or in the care, custody, and control of the insured. When this coverage is selected, it supersedes any other policy limitations shown in the policy for outdoor signs.

Interior Glass

This option covers glass items that are permanently attached to walls, ceilings, and floors of the building. When this option is selected, each glass item must specifically be described in the declarations, and this coverage supersedes any other policy limitations that refer to interior glass.

Employee Dishonesty

This option covers losses to business personal property, money, bullion, and securities as they pertain to acts of employees. Coverage does not apply to the insured or the insured's partners. The limit of insurance is listed on the declarations page. Losses must occur during the policy period or during the discovery period, which lasts for one year following the expiration of the policy.

Mechanical Breakdown

This option applies to direct damage because of sudden and accidental breakdown of boiler and pressure vessels and certain types of air conditioning units. This option requires that the unit is owned by the insured, or is in the care, custody, and control of the insured at the insured's premises. Damage must be accidental and caused by an insured peril. Damage that occurs during testing or servicing of the unit is not covered.

Burglary and Robbery (Standard Form Only)

This option covers business personal property, money, and securities loss due to burglary or robbery that occurs on or off the premises. Business personal property is limited to 25% of the business personal property amount that is shown in the declarations.

Money and Securities (Special Form Only)

This option covers the loss of money and securities against theft, disappearance and destruction. Money and securities must be used in the insured's business and be safely stored in a bank, at the insured's premises, the residence of the insured, or at the insured's partners or employees' locations, or at another location while they are being moved between these locations. The declarations page will list separate limits for money and securities that are stored on and off the premises.

Endorsements

The BOP was designed as an insurance package policy specifically to cover the needs of small businesses. Since these types of businesses vary, additional coverages are available that are tailored to the needs of specific business practices. All BOP policies provide standard coverage. Available endorsements include the following.

Utility Services-Direct Damage Coverage

The **Utility Services-Direct Damage Coverage** is an endorsement that covers direct loss or damage to business personal property that is caused by an interruption in water, communication, or power supply utilities. The business personal property must be scheduled and described on the policy to be covered as a loss, and the loss must be an insured peril.

Time Element Coverage

The **Time Element Coverage** endorsement is similar to The Utility Services-Direct Damage Coverage endorsement, except that it covers business income and extra expense that is lost due to an interruption in utility services. Here's an example of how these endorsements apply coverage:

> The insured owns a Laundromat business, and the washing machines and dryers are described and listed on the declarations page of the BOP. The insured added The Utility Services-Direct Damage and Time Element endorsements to the policy. An electrical transformer was struck by lightning causing a power surge. If the power surge damaged the machines, they would be covered under The Utility Services-Direct Damage endorsement. If the machines were not damaged during the surge, but the business had to close for two days because of a power outage, the Time Element endorsement would cover the lost income.

Protective Safeguards

The **Protective Safeguards** endorsement requires the insured to maintain the protective devices or systems listed on the endorsement as a condition of the policy, in order to cover loss due to fire. The insured is required to keep the protective safeguards in proper working order and must notify the insurer if the protective safeguard is not in working order. If an automatic sprinkler is shut off because of breakage, leakage, freezing, or opening of sprinkler heads and can be successfully repaired within 48 hours, the insured is not required to notify the insurer.

The protective safeguards are classified into the following categories:

- **P-1 Automatic sprinkler system**: This classification refers to a business property that has any automatic fire protective system, including related supervisory services and connected sprinklers, discharge nozzles, pipes, ducts, pumps, and similar devices.
- **P-2 Automatic fire alarm system**: This classification applies when the insured's property has an installed automatic fire alarm system that protects the entire building. It sends an automatic alarm to a central station or to a public or private fire alarm station.
- **P-3 Security service**: This classification applies when an insured contracts with a security service that employs a guard on the premises to make hourly rounds of the premises while the business is closed. There must be a recording system or watch clock.
- **P-4 Service contract**: This classification applies when an insured contracts with a privately-owned fire department that provides fire protection service to the premises.
- **P-9**: This classification applies when the property has any other protective system that is described in the endorsement.

Hired and non-owned auto liability is an endorsement that can be added to the BOP that covers hired or non-owned autos that are used by the business when the insured does not have a commercial auto policy in force. A **non-owned auto** is a vehicle that is being used for the insured's business but is not owned or rented by the insured. **A hired auto** is an auto that is leased, hired, or borrowed by the insured by someone other than his or her family or workers.

The insured or the insured's employees that use or maintain a hired or non-owned auto must be performing functions of the insured's business to be covered under the policy.

Other Features of a BOP

Replacement cost coverage is covered as part of the BOP, as long as the property is insured at 80% or more of the full replacement cost at the time of the loss.

Inflation guard coverage automatically increases the limit of insurance on a percentage basis and is available for both buildings and property. The applicable increase is represented as a percentage. Coverage is increased by the stated percentage on each renewal date. If a mid-term loss occurs, a pro rata adjustment is calculated based on the number of days the policy has been in force since the inception of the policy—or when the last limit of insurance was changed—divided by 365. For example, the limit of insurance is $100,000 with an inflation guard coverage percentage of 8%. If the number of days since the inception date of the policy at the time of the loss is 146, the calculation would be $100,000 X 0.08 X 146/365 which equals a $3,200 increase in the coverage limit.

The **control of property** condition regulates situations that are beyond the control of the insured. It is a condition of the policy that states an act of neglect by a person who is beyond the insured's direction or control will have no effect on the insurance. This condition also prevents an insured from voiding coverage for other locations if an insured has violated a condition of the policy with regard to one, specific location.

The **legal action against the insurer** condition limits the insured from bringing legal action against the insurer to within two years from the date that direct physical loss occurred. The insured must comply with all other conditions of the policy in order to bring legal action against the insurer.

Other Types of Commercial Policies

Transit Insurance

Transit insurance can cover property or property and liability. There are many forms of transit policies that cover goods or merchandise while it is being transported over land, sea, or air. Transit insurance can cover the shipper and/or the receiver, and bailees. **Trip transit** insurance covers a single shipment.

Motor truck cargo insurance is a type of inland marine insurance. It covers missing property while it is in transit. It can be written for goods that are transported via common carrier or for goods that are transported in the business owner's own vehicle. The **motor truck cargo-shipper's form** covers direct loss for shippers who carry their own goods. The **motor truck cargo-combination form** covers direct loss and liability coverage

An **annual transit policy** covers goods in transit for named or open perils for the shipper and receiver for all shipments made over a one-year period. A **bailee customer policy** covers property in the possession of a bailee. A **bailee** is in the business of storing, repairing, or servicing a customer's property. An example of this would be a tailor whose shop catches on fire, and customers' clothing is burned.

Ocean Marine Insurance

Ocean marine insurance was first developed as part of maritime loan policies in early Greek and Roman shipping industries. This makes it the oldest form of insurance. Ocean marine insurance covers goods and merchandise that are transported over domestic or international waters. Ocean marine insurance can be connected to inland marine and aviation transit coverage forms, where multiple forms of transportation are being used for the same shipment of goods and merchandise.

Coverages

Policies may be written on named peril or open-peril forms. In addition to fire and explosion, ocean marine policy perils cover risks that are germane to ocean transit. Such perils include pilferage, damage from ship condensation, and damage from contact with other cargo. It also includes perils of the sea, such as damage from strong winds, waves, or lightning. The policy also covers vessels that are stranded or immobilized due to sinking or collision, jettison—cargo that is dropped somewhere to protect the rest of the cargo, and barratry—deliberate damage from the ship's crew.

Ocean Marine Forms

Ocean marine insurance includes four forms:

- **Hull coverage** protects the owner of a ship or fleet of ships when the ship sustains physical damage due to a covered loss.

- **Cargo coverage** provides coverage for goods or merchandise while it is being transported over the sea. Coverage can be extended to cover cargo that is warehoused at the site of the shipper and receiver.

- **Freight coverage** pays the revenue that is owed to the ship's owner if cargo is damaged or destroyed due to an insured peril prior to arriving at the final destination. Freight insurance can be attached to hull or cargo insurance, or it can stand on its own policy.

- **Liability coverage** covers bodily injury and property damage arising out of the premises, operations, products, or completed operations that are related to the ocean marine policy.

Categories of Ocean Marine Property

The National Association of Insurance Commissioners (NAIC) adopted the **Nationwide Marine Insurance Definition,** which specifies the types of property that can be insured on inland or ocean marine insurance policies. The general criteria states that the property must be moveable, be in transit, or bear a relationship to being transported or communicated. The nationwide definition includes six categories of risks:

- Imports
- Exports
- Personal property floater risks
- Domestic shipments
- Instrumentalities of transportation or communication
- Commercial property floater risks

Loss Settlement

Some ocean marine policies contain a coinsurance clause. A 70% coinsurance clause means that the insurer would pay 70% of the value of a loss. A jettison loss is shared equally between every property owner and the ship owner.

Warranties

The insured must meet the conditions of the warranty in order to be compensated for loss. Ocean marine insurance policy warranties may be expressed or implied. **Expressed warranties** are stated in the policy and may contain exclusions for war, riots, or acts of civil commotion. An example of this would be if a policy states that a vessel will only be operated in the Caribbean Islands, but the vessel sails out of that area and has a loss. The insurer would likely decline coverage as the insured breached the warranty by operating it outside of the territory that is stated on the declarations page.

Implied warranties are not written into the policy, but because they reflect public and safety standards, they are enforceable as a policy condition. The insurer may decline a loss for vessels that are not seaworthy, contain poorly packaged cargo, detour from the designate route, or operate illegally.

Protection and Indemnity Insurance (P & I)

P & I insurance is a type of catchall insurance that covers liability for marine-related incidents that are not covered by workers' compensation or other parts of the ocean marine policy. This includes sailors who sustain work-related injuries, injuries to harbor and dock workers, and damage to cargo due to negligence. Since this is an indemnity policy, the insured must be legally responsible for damage in order for the insurer to pay.

Farm Insurance

Farm property insurance is also referred to as **farm and ranch owners' insurance**. Farm insurance is unique in that it covers the farmer's home, which is located on the farm, as well as the farmer's farm and farming operations. Farm insurance can be issued as a stand-alone policy or as part of a commercial package policy. It includes the homeowner's property, commercial property, and commercial liability coverages.

Coverages available in addition to the farmer's house include barns and other structures on the property: silos, livestock, feed, grain, produce, fertilizers, chemicals, farm machinery, equipment, tools, parts, contents used in farming operations, and farm liability. Additional coverages that may be available by endorsement for an additional premium include replacement cost of farm machinery and related items, feedlot liability, loss of use of farm machinery, milk contamination, and coverage for boarding and training of horses.

Like other personal and commercial policies, farm insurance can be issued in basic, broad, or special forms. Broad and special forms include perils that threaten livestock, such as animal attacks, electrocution, drowning, and accidental shooting. It also covers loading and unloading accidents. All farm vehicles must be specified on the policy to be covered.

Farm policies also have important exclusions including injuries to farm employees, aircraft spraying and pollutants, products of farm or farmer, and the farmer's actions or failure to act.

Fidelity Bonds

Fidelity bonds are purchased to protect employers from acts of dishonesty or theft by their employees. Fidelity bonds are three-party bonds—the insurance company, the employer, and the employee. However, the contractual obligation exists only between the insurance company and the employer, whereby the insurance company will pay for damages as the result of the actions of the employee.

Surety Bonds

Surety bonds are purchased to allow for coverage when a contractual obligation is not met or is unsatisfactory in regard to performance. Surety bonds are three-party bonds—the principal, obligor, and obligee. The **principal** is under a contractual obligation, the **obligee** is the party paying the principal for the contract, and the **obligor** is the insurance company who promises to pay if the principal fails to deliver on the contract. Even though the purchaser of a surety bond is the principal, the principal cannot collect any monies from the bond. The insurance company pays the obligee. Since the obligor is required to pay the obligee under the terms of the surety bond, this is one rare exception where misrepresentation on the part of the principal will not void coverage. Due to this provision, insurance companies will generally not issue a surety bond that totals more than the principal's assets so that they have a reasonable expectation to be successful in subrogating against the principal in the event they have to pay a claim. For this reason, the principal must provide detailed financial information to the insurance company and will be subject to in-depth investigation, such as the contractor's credit worthiness and reputation in regard to other work performed.

Other Types of Bonds

There are several other types of bonds issued by insurance company. They include the following:

- **Maintenance bond**: Guarantees the work performed by a principal after the work has been completed, usually issued for a period of one year
- **Performance bond**: Guarantees the principal will complete the work, including the insurance company hiring another principal to complete the job if the principals fails to complete the work
- **Payment bond**: Guarantees that all workers and subcontractors of the principal will be paid
- **Ancillary bond**: Guarantees that provisions in the contract not related to performance are satisfactorily completed
- **Bid bond**: Guarantees the principal will actually sign the contract and purchase any required bonds

Aviation Insurance

Aviation insurance is a specialty insurance coverage which requires sales and servicing by insurance experts in the aviation insurance field. Aviation insurance includes aircraft hull coverage which protects the aircraft from loss due to damage. Airport liability coverage covers accidents and occurrences at the airport. This includes coverage for passengers.

Other Insurance Types

Boat insurance or **yacht policies** cover open perils for physical damage to the boat and motor, liability, and medical payments up to the policy limits. Some policies will also include the boat trailer. It can also include personal effects, ski equipment, and fishing equipment. Policies generally settle losses on an actual cash value basis, and the policy may be endorsed to add coverage at replacement value.

Policies must state the territory where the boat is operated. Boats must be used for pleasure use and may not be used in exchange for a fee, boat charters for a fee, or racing in an official contest. Smaller boats may be able to be added to some homeowner insurance policies.

Personal watercraft refers to jet skis, Sea-doos, and waverunners. They may be insured on a stand-alone policy or added to some home insurance policies.

Motorcycle, snowmobile, recreational vehicle and ATV insurance covers the vehicle for liability and medical payments. Coverage can be added for physical damage of the vehicle. Claims are usually paid at actual cash value and coverage can sometimes be added to include replacement cost. Other endorsements may be offered to include equipment such as helmets, safety gear, and passenger liability.

Event insurance is sometimes required by private or public facilities where personal or commercial events are being held. Coverage includes liability and medical payments, and liquor liability may be added onto some policies. An example of this would be a wedding at a public or private establishment where the venue requires liability insurance, and the host is serving liquor. Some types of wedding insurance include lost deposits for jewelry, flowers, clothing and other items.

Trip cancellation insurance covers people who make large deposits on trips or vacations and have to cancel the trip due to an accident or illness. Trip cancellation policies are stand-alone policies issued on a per trip basis.

Types of Insurers

Insurance companies are classified by how they are owned, whether the company profits, and how any profits are managed. The most common types of insurance providers are **stock companies** and **mutual companies**. All insurance companies must have a calculated amount of guaranteed funds that will cover anticipated claims known as **reserves**. These fund amounts are calculated based on an insurance company's book of business. When a claim is filed, there must be a certain amount held in reserve until the claim is settled. For example, a claim is reported, and the **anticipated maximum claim settlement**—based on a number of factors, including historical settlements of claims of the same nature—is $500,000. The insurance company must allot $500,000 of their reserves specifically for that claim until the claim is settled.

Stock companies refers to a type of insurance company owned by shareholders. Stock companies operate by using money from the insureds' premiums and money that is generated by publicly trading stock. Stock companies don't require that their shareholders purchase insurance from their company. Shareholders can purchase insurance from any company they choose.

Mutual companies do not have shareholders and are also known as **cooperatives. Mutual insurance companies** refers to a type of insurance company owned by the policyholders. As partial owners of the insurance company, policyholders have the opportunity to vote on management decisions.

Policyholders are entitled to receive dividends from the insurance company, which represent the unearned portion of the premiums they pay.

Mutual insurance companies are subject to different statutory laws among the states. Mutual insurance companies may operate as advance premium insurers or assessment insurers. Most mutual insurance companies operate as advance premium insurers. A mutual insurance company that operates as an **advance premium insurer** assesses premiums in advance, and the premiums hold steady for some length of time. A mutual insurance company that operates as an **assessment insurer** assesses premiums based upon the actual experience of the company. Insureds pay a pro-rated share to cover the insurance company's costs. Assessment insurers have a high degree of variability and unpredictability in their costs of coverage, which makes this type of coverage less common than advance premium insurers. For these reasons, assessment insurers primarily offer only fire and windstorm protection for properties located in rural areas.

Reciprocal companies are also known as **exchanges**—comprised of an unincorporated group of people where the members are known as **subscribers**. The subscribers are responsible for paying premiums to a pool and sharing insurance costs and losses that are incurred by its members. An attorney-in-fact manages the exchange and all of its business. In the event that the premiums are not enough to cover a loss, a premium is assessed to all subscribers.

Fraternal benefit societies provide insurance for individuals who are members of a society. Typical examples include religious orders, lodges, and charitable benefit societies. In most cases, they only offer life and health insurance. Fraternal benefit societies are incorporated, but they do not operate for profit and do not offer stock. Fraternal benefit societies use open contracts that include the society's charter, bylaws, and amendments. A fraternal benefit society must continue to offer insurance benefits even if the charter is amended.

Lloyd's of London is an insurance market that is located in London's primary financial district and has been in existence since 1871. It is not a company, but a group of financial backers functioning as a **syndicate** who pool their resources to insure contracts. Lloyd's provides insurance to more than 200 countries and territories worldwide. It's similar to a reciprocal company where a group of syndicates join to pool and spread risk. Members of the syndicates are personally responsible for the insurance limits they assume. Lloyd's policies typically specialize in a unique type of risk, such as healthcare or agriculture, where a large loss would put a smaller insurer out of business. Lloyd's offers general insurance and **reinsurance**—insurance purchased by an insurance company. Risks that have been insured by Lloyd's include Keith Richard's fingers, Celine Dion's vocal chords, the development of the new World Trade Center in New York, and a portrait of the Queen and the Duke of Edinburgh engraved on a grain of rice.

Self insurers are organizations and individuals who cover their own losses using their own resources. These are generally wealthy individuals who can insure their own homes or other property. Another example would be large trade unions that have many members and self-insure for health insurance for the entire group. They are permitted to self-insure except where insurance is required by law, such as a personal automobile.

Risk-retention groups, created in 1986, are groups where each member of the group collectively insures large numbers of insurable units that are alike. They only insure liability loss exposures. A typical scenario of risk retention groups is when multiple product manufacturers combine to protect themselves against product liability. They may form under a **captive insurance agency**—one company, rather than many—or self-insure themselves to spread the risks among members. Each member is responsible for a pro-rated share of potential loss. Each member must be licensed in a minimum of one state where they conduct business, and the risk retention group is regulated in the state where it originates.

A **purchasing group** is a group of similar businesses that operate in the same trade or industry to purchase liability insurance. Like a risk-retention group, a purchasing group may operate in more than one state.

Government insurance is provided by state or federal governments to insure people against unemployment, worker injuries, disability, medical malpractice, and property damage. The federal government subsidizes state funds for catastrophes such as floods, hurricanes, and tornadoes.

Domicile of the Insurance Company

The **domicile** is the location where the insurer is permitted to do business. There are three types of domiciles:

- **Domestic:** insurer is headquartered in the state that it does business in
- **Foreign:** insurer is headquartered in another state
- **Alien:** insurer is headquartered in another country

Admitted and Non-Admitted Insurers

An **admitted insurer** may be a domestic, foreign, or alien insurer. In order for an insurer to be admitted, the state's insurance commissioner must issue the insurer a Certificate of Authority, permitting them to transact business in that state. The insurer must comply with all state insurance regulations. The state will take responsibility for making payments for insurance claims if the insurer defaults or goes out of business.

There are benefits to purchasing insurance from an admitted insurance carrier. The insured does not have to pay extra fees and taxes. This is due to having some protections that are afforded by having status as an admitted insurer. There is no risk to the insured when there is a large loss because insureds have full protection that is backed by the state insurance commission. Insureds also have the benefit of being able to file a complaint or appeal to the state insurance department.

Insuring with a non-admitted insurer carries far more risk than insuring with an admitted insurer. **Non-admitted insurance** carriers have not been approved by any state insurance department. There are no protections for insureds who contract with non-admitted insurers because non-admitted insurers are not required to comply with state insurance regulations. If the insurer fails to pay a claim or becomes insolvent, there is no guarantee of the state insurance commission or any other entity that the claim will be paid, even if the loss occurred prior to the time of bankruptcy or financial failure. There is no course of action to file an appeal if a claim was improperly handled.

On the surface, it appears that there is more security in insuring with an admitted insurer, but that is not necessarily the case. In addition to being either admitted or non-admitted with a state, insurers are graded according to their financial strength and stability. **A.M. Best** is the oldest and most widely-recognized organization that rates and reviews the financial data of the insurance industry. A.M. Best rates each insurer annually with a rating from A++ to F. It may be riskier to insure with an admitted insurer with a C rating than to insure with an A+ rated insurer that is non-admitted.

Insurance Companies

In addition to understanding insurance, the exam covers the structure of insurance agencies, insurance marketing and selling, underwriting, mandatory and optional insurance policy provisions, and legal considerations.

Functions of Insurance Companies

It's important for insurance agents and producers to understand every aspect of operating an insurance agency. Insurance agencies have responsibility for three main operational functions—actuarial, sales and marketing, and underwriting.

An **insurance agent** or **producer** is the front-line person who selects, classifies, and accepts risks on behalf of an insurer.

An **actuary** analyzes the probability of loss using math, statistics, demographics, marketing material, and financial theory. **Actuarial departments** use statistical tables and other data to properly assess and set rates for all types of risks.

The **sales and marketing** activities of an insurance agency provide for the distribution of products offered by the insurer or insurers. This includes explaining products and rate structures, preparing applications, collecting premiums, delivering the policies, and servicing existing policies.

Underwriters play an important part in risk selection. They apply the appropriate risk factors and ratings as determined by the actuarial department and guard against adverse selection. The underwriter assesses the potential risk based upon a prospective insured's application.

Policy Ratings

The **Insurance Services Office (ISO)** in Washington D.C. compiles actuarial data concerning property and casualty rates for the following lines of insurance:

- Homeowners
- Personal auto insurance
- Commercial general liability
- Commercial auto insurance
- Commercial property
- Commercial package policy
- Commercial inland marine
- Commercial umbrella
- Crime and fidelity
- Business owners

Insurance Policy

An **insurance policy** is a formal contract between the insurer and the insured that **indemnifies**, or compensates, the insured for loss. The **insurance contract** sets forth the exact terms of the agreement, including the specific risks and perils that are covered, the effective dates of coverage, the amount of premium, the mode of premium, coverage exclusions, and **deductibles**. The agreement determines the types and amounts of claims that the insurer is legally required to pay.

Policy Process

The insurance agent gathers information about the insured and the type of property or casualty to be covered and presents it to an underwriter for review. Once the application is complete and signed, the insurance agent can bind coverage on behalf of the insurer. In most cases, the insurance agent can bind coverage in absence of a review of the risk. In addition, the insurance agent may bind coverage verbally. Whether an insurance agent can bind coverage in the absence of a review of the risk, and whether he or she can bind coverage verbally depends on the insurance agent's binding authority. Insurance agents issue three types of receipts when an insurance application is initially signed:

- **Conditional receipt:** The effective date is the same date as the application, unless the application is declined for an acceptable reason.
- **Unconditional receipt:** Also known as a temporary insurance agreement, the coverage becomes effective immediately upon the insured paying an initial premium. Coverage lasts for a fixed period of time, regardless whether the insurer accepts the application.
- **Acceptance receipt:** Coverage becomes effective on the date that the application is accepted.

Any insurance policy can be declared null and void, meaning it never existed, if it is found that the insured engaged in misrepresentation, meaning he or she failed to provide information—or provided falsified information—on the application.

Reinsurance

Reinsurance is a common practice where one insurer transfers portions of risk portfolios to another insurer to act as a financial safety net in the event of a catastrophic claim. **Reinsurance** is also known as **insurance for insurers** or **stop-loss insurance**.

Insurers use actuarial data to determine how much they are likely to pay out in the event of a loss. Based upon that data, insurers set a retention limit, which is the maximum amount of risk that the insurer can retain without risk of insolvency. Because of the catastrophic nature of claims, losses can be much larger than insurers anticipate. Many insurers purchase insurance from other insurance companies as a way to financially manage risks for catastrophic losses to reduce their risk. The insurer **cedes**, or assigns, amounts beyond their retention limit to a reinsurer. When an insurer cedes risk to more than one insurer for the purpose of reinsurance, the group of reinsurers is called a **syndicate**.

In a reinsurance agreement, the insurer becomes the **cedent,** meaning the one who passes the financial obligation to another, and the insurance company that the insurer purchases insurance coverage from becomes the **reinsurer**. The transfer agreement can be made directly between the cedent and reinsurer or arranged through a broker.

Reinsurance agreements may be automatic or **facultative**, meaning optional. In an **automatic agreement**, the excess risk is automatically ceded to a reinsurer or syndicate, without examination. In a **facultative agreement**, the reinsurer may re-underwrite the risk and attach additional conditions that the insurer must attach to the final, binding policy.

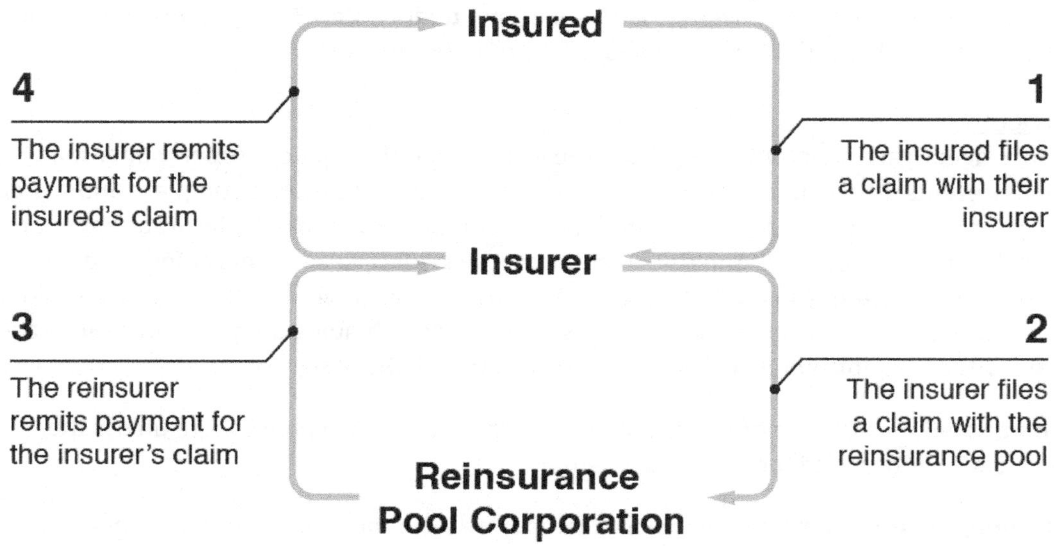

The Insurance Contract-Mandatory (Standard) Policy Provisions

State laws require that issued policies contain certain **mandatory or standard provisions**. They include the following:

- **Entire contract clause**: A protection for the insured that limits the insurance agreement to the provisions found in the contract, such as the policy form, conditions, amendments, endorsements, and a copy of the application
- **Incontestability clause**: A clause that prevents the insurer from voiding the contract for a certain period of time, due to a misstatement by the insured, typically has two years for the insurer to contest any material statements
- **Grace period**: The amount of time that the policy extends without lapse, when the insured has not made a timely payment of the premium
- **Reinstatement period**: A period of time where insurance coverage can be reestablished, may include evidence of eligibility and payment of past and current premiums
- **Notice of claim provision**: Also called **notice of loss**, a notice to the insurer, through the insurance agent, the insured, or a third party, that a claim has occurred, can be given in writing or by phone; if insured is injured or otherwise incapacitated, notice of claim can occur as soon as possible after the insured is able to file notice of claim
- **Claim form**: A document that provides information on the loss that occurred and is required by an insurer

- **Proof of loss form**: Any documents that demonstrate that a loss occurred—e.g., medical bills, police reports, receipts for temporary damage to a home, towing bills, and receipts for damaged property

- **Time payment of claims provision**: Refers to the timely payment of claims required by insurers as provided for based upon the terms that the insurer set in the policy wording

- **Legal action provision**: In most standard insurance coverage forms may also be stated as **legal action against us**, outlines the legal rights and responsibilities of insureds before exercising their rights to sue the insurer for enforcement of the policy. This may include imposing limitations for the insureds. A typical timeframe requires the insured to wait 60 days from the date a claim was declined before filing legal action or limiting time to file action to within three years, after the 60-day waiting period. Some liability policies include legal action against insurer clauses that state that third-party beneficiaries cannot sue the insurer for damages being sought against an insured.

In addition to the policy provisions that are required by law, the insurer may include **optional policy provisions,** for the purpose of protecting their interests. Common optional policy provisions include the following:

- **Misstatement of age or gender** is something that can have a substantial impact on rating. It is listed as an optional policy provision to allow the insurer the opportunity to adjust the policy's premium based upon the correct age of the insured, as provided on the policy application. Using the correct information, the insurer may adjust the premium higher or lower and provide for a refund if premiums were overpaid. Also as part of this provision, the gender of an insured can have a substantial impact with regard to rating, particularly for automobile policies. This provision allows the insurer to make premium adjustments according to gender. With regard to age and gender, this provision allows the insured to make premium adjustments without having to invoke the incontestability clause.

- The **other insurance with this carrier provision** prevents a situation where someone or something is over-insured. When an insured has more than one policy in force for the same coverage, this provision allows one of the insurers to be primary coverage over the other one. The insurer can designate that they provide no coverage when other insurance is in place, pay a pro-rated share, or apply coverage in excess of the primary insurer.

- The **unpaid premiums provision** holds that when an insured fails to pay premiums beyond the grace period, the policy will lapse. If a loss occurs during the grace period, the benefit is paid minus the amount of the outstanding premium. If a loss occurs beyond the grace period and enters a true lapse period, there is no coverage, and no claims will be paid.

- The **conformity with state statutes provision** is a provision that assures that the policy conforms to the state statutes in the state where the policy is issued. It's not uncommon for insurers to offer policies in multiple states. Rather than write a new contract for each state, the conformity with state stature clause ensures that all optional provisions conform to the state statutes of the state where the policy is being issued, in addition to the mandatory provisions. The conformity with state statutes clause is included so that insurers are not at risk of non-compliance with any state's minimum statutory requirements.

    For example, if an insurer offers a policy in a state where the state minimum automobile insurance limits are $20,000 per person, $40,000 per accident, and $15,000 for property damage, and the insurer issues the same policy in another state, where the state minimum automobile insurance limits are $25,000 per person, $50,000 per accident, and $20,000 for property damage, the insurer is legally required to pay the higher limits.

- The **illegal act provision** excludes certain coverage for certain acts that are deemed illegal or being in violation of the law. This is also considered a **moral hazard**. An example of this is when a third party steals a car or borrows it without permission from the owner and gets into an accident where another party is injured, and there is property damage. The insured's policy could refuse to pay damages because the driver performed an illegal act. In this case, the insured could sue the driver directly for the damages.
- An **exclusion for intoxicants and narcotics** is an optional provision and is sometimes referred to as a **substance abuse exclusion**. A policy that contains this provision allows insurers to exclude losses that result from the use of drugs and alcohol. An example of this would be an insured who becomes inebriated at a party and damages property at the host's house. The insurer for the insured could refuse to cover the loss due to the insured's consumption of excess alcohol.
- A **cancellation provision** allows an insurer to cancel or non-renew an insurance policy for a stated reason other than non-payment of premium by sending a notice of cancellation. The cancellation provision will state the number of days of notice that the insurer will give to the insured if the policy will be cancelled. Typically, it will be 30 or 60 days, as defined in a state statute. Depending upon the reason for cancellation and jurisdiction, some insurers require advance notice of cancellation or non-renewal between 10 and 75 days. The insured may choose not to pay the renewal premium, which would constitute non-renewal of the insurance policy.

Legal Considerations

The insurance contract is legally enforceable in a court of law. It is a contract between two parties, the insurer and the insured, or policy owner, where the insurer grants rights to the policy owner who has an insurable interest in a business or property.

Five elements must be present in order for an insurance contract to be considered legally binding. Without any one of them, the contract is considered to be void:

- Offer
- Acceptance
- Consideration

- Legal competence
- Legal purpose

After a potential insured has reviewed an insurance proposal, the next step is to complete the application and make an initial payment. This constitutes the **offer**.

When the insurance company accepts the offer and agrees to issue the policy, this is called **acceptance**. The insurer may decide to make some changes to the proposed terms before accepting the offer. For example, the insurer may request a higher deductible if the insured has filed recent claims.

Each party to the contract is required to give **valuable consideration**. On the part of the applicant, part of the consideration pertains to the accuracy of the information that is stated on the contract. This is important because the insurer relies on that information explicitly when making the decision to accept the offer. The applicant also provides value with the obligation of paying current and future premiums. With regard to the insurer, consideration refers to the obligations contained in the policy contract and the money they pay out in the event of a loss.

The potential insured needs to be legally competent to enter into an insurance contract.

Competency refers to whether an individual has a mental illness or developmental disability that renders them incapable of understanding the terms of a contract. Being **legally incompetent** also refers to an individual who has not reached the majority age in the state of policy issuance. With regard to insurers, they are deemed competent if they are licensed under the prevailing governmental regulations.

A contract must be written for a **legal purpose** in order for it to be legally binding. Any contract that would not be legally enforceable in a civil court for breach of contract—even if the other elements of a legally binding contract applied—would render the contract illegal.

Representations and Warranties

During the discussion between the agent and a proposed insured, the proposed insured makes statements about personal information, the property to be insured, and the type of liability needed. These statements form the basis for which the insurer makes an underwriting decision and issues an insurance policy. Those statements can be classified as **representations** or **warranties.**

A **representation** is a presentation of fact—either by words or by conduct—that entices someone to act. For the purpose of insurance, a representation induces the insurer to enter into a contract with a proposed insured. An example of a representation is that a man and woman state their names as first and second named insured and state that they are married. If this representation was later found to be untrue, it would be considered a **misrepresentation**.

Misrepresentation, Concealment, and Fraud

Insurers have the right to cancel or null and void a policy or deny a claim when it is discovered that an insured intentionally misrepresents or conceals material facts in the insurance application. When a deliberate misrepresentation or concealment is made during the application process, it gives the insurer the right to cancel or null and void the policy. When misrepresentations or concealments are made after policy issuance and during the claims process, the insurer has the right to deny payment for the claim.

Misrepresentation refers to false statements made by an insured. If the misrepresented statement refers to matters that are factored into an insured's decision to consider and issue the policy, the insurer may decide to cancel the policy, while staying on the risk for a specified amount of time, usually two weeks, during which time they will be obligated to pay for any eligible losses. They may also decide to null and void the policy, meaning the policy never existed and, therefore, no claims of any kind will be made.

Usually the decision whether to cancel or null and void an insurance policy is based on the severity of the misrepresentation. For example, an applicant for a tenant's personal property insurance application by a 70-year-old woman indicates she has had no property claims in the last six years, but a prior insurance check reveals two claims in the last six years—a misrepresentation. The claims experience makes the risk ineligible for insurance in the regular market with the insurance company, but due to the fact that the woman may have simply forgotten about the claims, the insurance company may choose to stay on the risk for a period of fourteen days, giving the woman time to place the tenant's insurance in another market.

In another example, a male seeking personal auto insurance states that he is 25 years old with no claims or moving violations in the past six years. The underwriter discovers the male is actually 21 years old and has had one at-fault accident, two speeding tickets, and had his license suspended for a period of six months in the past five years. The applicant is ineligible for insurance in the regular market, and it is perceived that he was trying to deceive the insurance company in order to gain a favorable premium, a case of blatant misrepresentation. In this case, the insurance company would likely null and void the policy, meaning the policy never existed and, as such, no claims would be paid.

Concealment is deliberately withholding information or material facts for the purpose of securing an insurance policy. Deliberate concealment that is discovered will most likely result in the policy being null and void.

Fraud is the most serious action with regard to deceiving an insurer and includes concealing or misrepresenting facts with intent to cause harm or injury. For the purpose of insurance, this means receiving benefits through a claim that the insured would otherwise not be entitled to. An example would be if an insured was proven to have burned down his personal residence or purposely driven his vehicle into a lake in a fraudulent attempt to submit a bogus claim—in order to collect money from the insurance company. Investigators, such as those determining the cause of fires, are very adept at detecting fraud. In cases where an insured is guilty of arson on his own home, for example, it is often noted that family photos have been removed from the walls as have any expensive and portable electronics.

Legal Interpretations Related to Insurance Contracts

Disagreements about insurance contracts fall under tort law and contract law. The specific type of contract further defines **legal interpretations**. Here are some different types of contracts:

- **Contract of adhesion**: A contract where the insurer presents terms and conditions to an insured without room for negotiation
- **Aleatory contract**: A contract where the parties are not required to act until the occurrence of a particular event

- **Conditional contract**: Also known as a **hypothetical contract**, requires that another agreement is performed, or another condition be satisfied in order for the contract to be considered enforceable
- **Contract of indemnity**: A contract where an insured receives the true value of the loss without any loss or gain
- **Personal contract**: A contract where the insured person has insurable interest, and coverage cannot be transferred to another individual
- **Unilateral contract**: A contract between legally competent parties to do or refrain from doing specified acts and where one party pays the other party to perform a duty

Waiver and Estoppel

Insurance contracts contain rights and provisions for both parties. A **waiver** is the act of a party forgoing or waiving a right or privilege outlined in the contract. Waivers are often used to acquire coverage or reduce premium for coverage. For example, if a house has an older style chimney that would normally result in a higher premium being charged, the owner may declare the chimney is closed off and not in use. The insurance company may then elect not to charge the higher premium and coverage for any losses related to that chimney would be waived, meaning those losses would not be covered by the insurance company.

Estoppel prevents an individual or organization from changing a position, action, or attitude that is inconsistent with a position he or she took earlier if it would result in harm or injury to another person. A common example of this is when an insurer customarily accepts late payments during the grace period. Estoppel would prevent the insurer from suddenly deciding to cancel the policy during the grace period for non-payment of premium.

Types and Roles of Producers

A **producer** has a relationship with an insurer or insurers that details how insurance products are presented to a proposed insured and to the extent that the producer binds the insurer to the contract. Agents, brokers, and consultants are all producers. The differences between them is with regard to how they are compensated and whether they are obliged to serve the needs of the insured or the insurer.

Producers have three main responsibilities:

1. **Fiduciary duty**: To collect premiums, keep them separate from personal accounts, and remit them to the insurer in a timely manner

2. **Accurate submission of information**: To submit insurance applications that accurately reflect information that affects the insurer's decision to offer coverage

3. **Making product recommendations**: To explain insurance products to a proposed insured and make recommendations for policies that best serve the insured's needs

An **agent** contracts directly with an insurer and is legally obligated to work in the best interests of that insurer. **Captive**, or exclusive, agents are only permitted to sell products from the insurer that they contract with. Agents may refer to themselves as **brokers** when they represent more than one insurance vendor. Agents are usually compensated on a commission basis, though any combination of salary and commission is acceptable.

Brokers are also called **agents of record**. They typically represent more than one insurance vendor and are legally obliged to work on behalf of the insured. Brokers usually receive a commission from the insurers that they represent though any combination of salary and commission is acceptable.

Consultants provide insurance advice to clients without having any direct contracts or relationships with insurers. Consultants charge their own fees directly to their clients.

Surplus lines brokers are licensed and permitted to place insurance with non-admitted insurers. Surplus lines insurers may offer insurance products through a surplus lines broker that is licensed in the state where coverage is being written. Surplus lines insurers will insure risks that other insurers cannot or will not insure. Examples of this are distressed homes and insurance to cover a single event. Surplus lines insurers are paid a commission by the insurers they have contracts with.

The **law of agency** refers to a consensual relationship between the principal insurer and the agent, where the insurer grants authority to the agent to act on its behalf in dealing with a third party. The law of agency is a fiduciary relationship, and it binds the principal insurer to the actions of the agent.

Types of Authority

The contract between the principal insurer and the agent spells out the type of authority that the agent has. The agent may be given one of three types of authority.

- **Expressed authority**: Authority that the principal insurer gives to the agent, usually expressly written into the contract but can also be authority that is given to the agent orally
- **Implied authority**: Also known as **usual authority**, authority that an insured assumes that the agent has. An agent uses implied authority when doing things that are reasonably necessary to perform customary agent duties effectively.
- **Apparent authority**: An agent's power to act on behalf of a principal insurer, even in cases where express or implied authority was not granted; applies when a third party believes that the agent had authority, based upon the principal's conduct and protects third parties in cases where it is reasonable to think that the agent's signature bound the principal to cover a loss

Insurance Regulations

The insurance industry is regulated at the state and federal levels to protect insureds when their risks are transferred to an insurer.

Errors and Omissions (E & O) is a type of professional liability insurance that protects individuals who offer professional advice, such as doctors, lawyers, consultants, brokers, and insurance agents. It protects individuals in certain professions from bearing the full cost of defending a civil lawsuit, where the client alleges negligence, due to an error or omission. This may include failure of an insurance agent to provide an adequate insurance limit or failing to provide information about important conditions or exclusions.

Federal regulations protect consumers nationally to ensure that insurance practices are fair and reasonable and do not violate the rights of individuals. Here are a few important federal statutes:

- **Fair Credit Reporting Act of 1971 (FCRA)**: This law states that the insured is entitled to request and receive any credit and other reporting data used in the determination to issue or deny coverage.
- **McCarran-Ferguson Act of 1945**: This Act gives the right to regulate insurance matters to the states, unless the matters are regulated by federal law.
- **Gramm-Leach-Bliley Financial Modernization Act of 1999**: This act allows banks, securities, and insurance companies to participate in commercial and investment banking activities. In addition, the act regulates state minimum standards so that they do not interfere with federal laws.
- **Dodd-Frank Wall Street Reform and Consumer Protection Act of 2010**: This act was created by the Consumer Financial Protection Bureau (CFPB) to oversee the industries of securities, banking, and insurance.

Insurance laws are predominantly state-based and vary substantially as a result. The **National Association of Insurance Commissioners** (NAIC) was created as a national system of state-based insurance regulation. NAIC sets standards and regulatory support for insurers and consumers in the fifty states, the District of Columbia, and five U.S. territories. NAIC relies on chief insurance regulators from all members to establish standards, identify best practices, conduct peer reviews, and to regulate insurers. NAIC sets minimum capital levels for insurers to protect insureds from insurer insolvency, meaning an insurer that cannot pay the insured's claims.

The **doctrine of comity** is also known as **comity of states**. Comity refers to reciprocity, a principle by which one state defers its own laws to the laws of another state.

Many states have laws that require insurers to educate insureds with basic information about insurance. A **Buyer's Guide to Insurance** is usually specific to home or auto insurance. It usually includes information for contacting the state's insurance commission.

Insurers that do business in all fifty states, Puerto Rico, and the District of Columbia are required to be members of a **state insurance guaranty association (SIGA)**. When an insurer becomes insolvent and cannot pay its claims, the other members of the guaranty association are assessed a fee based upon their premium share to pay for claims that another insurer defaulted on. SIGAs may set caps on the amount that they will pay. Many states have one SIGA for life and health insurance and another for property and casualty insurance.

Terrorism Risk Insurance Act (TRIA)

Established in 2002 and later updated, the **Terrorism Risk Insurance Act** (TRIA) guarantees that insurance companies will offer insured's coverage against acts of intentional terrorism. Insurance companies cover the initial losses and are reimbursed by the government subject to deductibles and retention rates. Both foreign and domestic acts of terrorism are included. Exclusions apply to commercial autos, burglary, theft, surety, professional liability—other than directors and officers liability—and farm owners multiple peril.

Practice Questions

1. Farmer Jones grows corn and soybeans. He has a farm owner's property and liability policy. His family home sits on the property, as well as a barn. He lists all of his tractors and farming equipment on his policy. A late summer hailstorm ripped through the area and caused damage to the roof on his house. There was also damage to the barn and one tractor. One third of the soybean crop was destroyed. Which of the following are covered under the loss?
   a. The house, the barn, and loss of income from the soybeans only
   b. The tractor, the barn, and loss of income from the soybeans only
   c. The tractor, the barn, and the house only
   d. The house, the barn, the tractor, and the loss of income from the soybeans

2. Two college students rented an apartment that they share. Sandra took out a tenant policy, but Mary did not. They returned to the apartment after class and noticed that there had been a break-in, which damaged the entry door. They also noticed that some of Mary's property had been stolen, including a bicycle, an electronic tablet, and a leather jacket. Which items are covered under the loss on Sandra's tenant policy?
   a. The bicycle, the tablet, and the jacket only
   b. The door, the bicycle, the tablet, and the jacket
   c. The door only
   d. None of them

3. What is the best definition for reinsurance?
   a. Risk transfer
   b. Risk sharing
   c. Risk avoidance
   d. Risk retention

4. Which of the following characteristics does NOT apply to an insurable loss?
   a. Predictable
   b. Measurable
   c. Catastrophic
   d. Unexpected

5. An insured's private vehicle is parked in his driveway when a tree from his yard falls on the vehicle, causing damage. Which coverage on the insured's private auto policy would cover the loss?
   a. Collision
   b. Comprehensive
   c. Property damage liability
   d. Towing coverage

6. Which types of coverage forms include loss by theft?
   a. Broad and special only
   b. Broad and basic only
   c. Basic and special only
   d. Basic, broad, and special

7. Which type of insurer is managed by an attorney-in-fact?
   a. Stock
   b. Mutual
   c. Reciprocal
   d. Fraternal benefit society

8. What conditions must be met for robbery to be covered under a crime policy?
   a. Injury
   b. Threat of violence
   c. Theft of property
   d. Visual surveillance

9. Which type of business is NOT eligible for a business owner's policy (BOP)?
   a. Auto glass shop
   b. Delicatessen
   c. Electronics store
   d. Bar or tavern

10. Which of the following property parameters does NOT have to be met in order to qualify for inland marine insurance?
   a. Must be moveable
   b. Must be related to transportation or communication
   c. Must be in possession of a bailee
   d. Must be stored at an insured location

11. Which type of bond covers loss due to employee theft?
   a. Municipal bonds
   b. Fidelity bonds
   c. Surety bonds
   d. Fiduciary bonds

12. The physical damage that was sustained to an auto during a collision loss is calculated on what basis?
   a. Actual cash value
   b. Replacement value
   c. Fair market value
   d. Stated value

13. What type of liability is Errors and Omissions coverage?
   a. Professional liability
   b. Commercial liability
   c. Personal liability
   d. Excess liability

14. An insured homeowner purchases a new refrigerator and transports it to her home in the truck that she insures under her personal auto policy. During the trip home, the tailgate falls open, and the appliance crashes into the street, causing a total loss to the appliance. What type of coverage will pay for the loss?
    a. Inland Marine property
    b. Commercial auto property
    c. Business personal property
    d. Homeowner personal property

15. An owner of a condominium or cooperative building would need to purchase which policy form?
    a. HO-3
    b. HO-4
    c. HO-5
    d. HO-6

16. The replacement cost of a homeowner's home is $200,000, and the homeowner insures it for $150,000, with a $1,000 deductible. The home catches on fire and has a loss of $10,000. How much money will the homeowner receive at the time of loss settlement?
    a. -$8,333
    b. $10,000
    c. $8,375
    d. $9,000

17. A home is insured for $350,000. The home has a detached three-car garage on the property. How much is the garage insured for in the event of a loss?
    a. Replacement cost of the three-car garage
    b. Actual cash value of the three-car garage
    c. $35,000
    d. Nothing, because it is not attached to the house

18. Which of the following types of insurance is a licensed property that a casualty insurance agent or broker is NOT allowed to sell?
    a. Auto insurance
    b. Disability insurance
    c. Home insurance
    d. Commercial liability insurance

19. Which of the following is NOT considered to be part of a commercial package policy (CPP)?
    a. Commercial warehouse
    b. Commercial umbrella
    c. Machinery inside commercial buildings
    d. A van used for business purposes

20. Which of the following types of dwelling cannot be insured using a dwelling policy?
    a. Farmhouse and farm buildings
    b. Four-unit townhouse
    c. Single family home
    d. Mobile home

21. Which of the following terms describes a legal doctrine wherein a party cannot contradict their own previous actions if those actions have been reasonably relied on by another party, such as when an insurance company has accepted late monthly premiums from an insured for six consecutive months, but the insurance company then cancels the policy on the basis of late premiums in the seventh month?
    a. Waiver
    b. Estoppel
    c. Fraud
    d. Insurable interest

22. Which of the following is NOT part of an insurance contract?
    a. Consideration
    b. Legal intent
    c. Offer
    d. Warranty

23. Which of the following terms describes the peril that has the most significant impact resulting in a loss?
    a. Remote cause
    b. Probability of loss
    c. Proximate cause
    d. Occurrence

24. Under a reinsurance agreement, what financial obligation does the insurer have to insure a loss?
    a. 100% payment for the loss
    b. 50% payment for the loss
    c. An amount equal to the retention level
    d. No financial obligation

25. A new homeowner would most likely purchase which form of homeowner insurance?
    a. HO-2 OR HO3
    b. HO-4 OR HO5
    c. HO-4 OR HO6
    d. HO-1 OR HO4

26. David owns a single-family home and insured it under a DP-3 policy, and he added $10,000 for Coverage C, personal property. He rents it to a tenant on an annual lease. The tenant notified him that the clothes dryer in the basement caught on fire. It burned part of the wall and damaged the dryer. He was able to put out the fire and disconnect the dryer. What will the insurer pay for the loss?
    a. Nothing, fire is not a covered loss under a DP-3 form
    b. The full cost to repair the wall and actual cash value to repair or replace the dryer, minus deductible
    c. The full cost to repair the wall minus the deductible, but not the dryer
    d. The full cost to repair the wall and repair or replace the dryer, minus the deductible

27. Tracy purchased a distressed home on a foreclosure sale. She plans to rehab the home and either resell it or rent it out. She called several insurance companies, and they all refused to insure the home, due to its dilapidated condition. What kind of insurance agent can help her obtain a policy for this home until the renovation is completed?

a. A captive agent
b. A repurchasing agent
c. A surplus lines broker
d. A reciprocal insurer

28. A contractor completes work on a dwelling that is later found to be substandard and not up to code. The owner of the dwelling can make a claim to have the work corrected and any violations brought up to code. Under which bond would the owner of the dwelling make a claim?

a. Maintenance bond
b. Bid bond
c. Performance bond
d. Payment bond

29. Jacob is a business owner, who has a commercial package policy on his business. He heard on the news that a nearby forest was on fire and was spreading in the direction of his business. Firefighters tamed the blaze, but not before it scorched one acre of his property and damaged one building. How much will his insurer pay for the loss?

a. The cost to repair the building, but nothing for the lawn
b. The cost to repair the building and the cost to repair the lawn
c. The cost to repair the lawn, but nothing for the building
d. Nothing at all

30. Heavy rains came down in Mindy's area. She woke up to find her entire yard had standing water. She checked the basement and found a foot of water in the basement. Her sump pump was broken. The carpet was soaked, and her furniture was damaged. Which items will her homeowner's insurance form HO-5 pay for in this loss?

a. The cost to replace the sump pump, but not the carpet or furniture
b. The cost to replace the carpet and furniture, but not the repair of the sump pump
c. The cost to replace the sump pump, the carpet, and the furniture
d. Nothing

31. When completing an application for personal auto insurance, the applicant tells the insurance agent that he has had no auto claims in the past six years. Upon receiving the applicant's insurance history, the underwriting department discovers the applicant has had three claims in the past six years: two under liability where the insured was at fault for two accidents and one under comprehensive for a new windshield. Which of the following terms would best describe the fact that the insured neglected to tell the insurance agent about the three claims?

a. Fraud
b. Misrepresentation
c. Concealment
d. Rebating

32. In an HO-3 policy, which coverage pays for loss of use?
    a. Coverage B
    b. Coverage C
    c. Coverage A
    d. Coverage D

33. Stella attended a party and slipped on a banana peel, which caused her to fall and break her leg. She filed a claim against the host of the party for her medical bills and the ambulance ride. What is this type of claim called?
    a. Property claim
    b. Accident claim
    c. Tort claim
    d. Medical claim

34. John retired after working in the same factory for 25 years. A year later, John was having difficulty breathing, and his doctor informed him that testing showed John had been breathing in particles due to the asbestos present in the factory, permanently damaging his lungs. John presents a claim for his medical expenses to his former employer. Under which of the following terms would John's claim be considered?
    a. An event
    b. An occurrence
    c. An accident
    d. A claims-made trigger

35. Joan owns a hair salon, which she insures on a business owner's policy. She closed the shop when she went on vacation. When she returned, she noticed that a pipe had broken, causing water damage to the wall and the floor. The proximate cause of the loss was because she turned the heat off, and some unseasonably cold weather came in, causing the pipes to freeze. What will the policy cover for the loss?
    a. Nothing
    b. The full cost to repair the wall and the floor only
    c. The full cost of repairing the pipe, the wall, and the floor
    d. The cost of plumbing repairs only

36. Which of the following is NOT included on the declarations page of an insurance policy?
    a. The type of property
    b. The effective dates of the policy
    c. The exclusions
    d. The coverage limits

37. An insured files a claim for a covered loss on his building and personal property policy immediately after the loss. How many days does the insurer have to pay for the loss?
    a. 60 days
    b. 30 days
    c. 15 days
    d. There is no limit

38. Which of the following is NOT a party in a surety bond?
   a. Surety
   b. Obligee
   c. Principal
   d. Secondary

39. When the extension is added to insure newly-acquired or constructed property, which of the following are the maximum limits?
   a. $250,000 for the building and $250,000 for business personal property
   b. $250,000 for the building and $100,000 for business personal property
   c. $100,000 for the building and $250,000 for business personal property
   d. $100,000 for the building and $100,000 for business personal property

40. Which of the following bonds are ALL contracts between three parties and often purchased by contractors?
   a. Municipal, bail, fiduciary, utility bonds
   b. Performance, surety, bid, maintenance bonds
   c. Agency, fidelity, license, payment bonds
   d. Corporate, mortgage, freight, broker bonds

Answer Explanations

1. C: Hail is a covered loss under the policy. A farm owner's property policy covers a single-family home, in addition to farm buildings. Since the tractor was listed on the policy as scheduled farm property, it is also covered. Crops growing in a field are excluded on a farm policy, so they would not be covered. The farmer could have bought a separate policy for crop insurance.

2. D: There must be insurable interest for the policy to respond to the loss. Since Mary does not have a policy of her own, and she does not have insurable interest in Sandra's policy, there is no coverage for her stolen items. Sandra did not sustain a loss, nor suffer financially from a loss, so her policy would not pay on her behalf. The landlord's policy would cover the damage to the door.

3. A: Reinsurance is a common practice where one insurer transfers portions of risk portfolios to another insurer to act as a financial safety net in the event of a catastrophic claim. Risk sharing is when a risk is shared among many, such as when the premiums and losses are shared among a group of policy holders based on a certain formula. Risk avoidance is when an insurance company avoids or does not insure a risk as the expected rate of claims that would cover the risk would be too high. Risk retention means risks that are accepted or retained by an insurance company.

4. C: The six characteristics of insurable loss are the following: it must be predictable, must subject a large quantity of people or things to loss, must be unexpected, must be measurable, must be a randomly selected exposure, and cannot be catastrophic in nature. Loss exposures must be randomly selected. Catastrophic losses do not meet these characteristics.

5. B: Comprehensive coverage includes anything other than a collision. This includes falling objects, weather-related damage, glass breakage, and hitting an animal with the vehicle.

6. A: Basic forms only cover the W.C. SHAVER named perils, including windstorm, civil commotion, smoke, hail, aircraft, vehicles, explosion, and riot. The broad and special forms include coverage for theft.

7. C: A reciprocal insurer is comprised of an unincorporated group of people, or subscribers, which is also known as an exchange. The exchange is managed by an attorney-in-fact. Stock insurers, in addition to their reserve and surplus funds, are contributed to by stockbrokers who invest in a capital fund. Shares are usually traded on one of the official stock exchanges, like the Total System Services (TTS). Mutual insurers are owned and operated by insureds for the insureds' benefits. Every owner of the company is an insured. Every insured is an owner of the company. Frat Benefit Societies are an organization of people who are members of a common society that share a common vocational, ethnic, or religious affiliation. Frat Benefit Societies may be church related and are often engaged in the sale of life insurance.

8. B: Threat of violence must occur in order to be considered robbery. A loss where there was a break-in without the threat of violence would be considered a burglary. An injury does not have to occur in the event of a robbery. Theft of property does not have to happen in order for the incident to be considered a robbery. While visual surveillance may be present, it has no bearing on whether or not the incident is a robbery.

9. D: Bars, pubs, cocktail lounges, and taverns are not eligible for a business owner policy. Business owner policies include property and liability for certain types of small businesses that have less risk than large commercial businesses or businesses with higher risk. An establishment that serves alcohol has a higher risk of liability than a small sandwich shop, laundry service, or retail store.

10. D: One of the requirements to be considered commercial inland marine property is that it must be in transit. Commercial inland marine policies cover losses for commercial property (e.g., goods and products) that is transported over land and is not at a fixed location. Property must be in transit, must be moveable, must be related to transportation or communication, and must be in the possession of a bailee.

11. B: The word fidelity means honesty. Business owners whose employees handle or manage money will need fidelity bond or employee dishonesty insurance. It protects the employer from acts of theft of money, securities, and property that is owned or controlled by the employer. This coverage may be included as part of commercial crime policies.

12. A: The purpose of insurance is to indemnify—make the insured whole. Cars that suffer loss due to a collision are settled on an actual cash basis so that the insured gets the same value after the loss as the value the car had prior to the loss. If the loss was settled on a replacement or stated value, the insured would likely get more for the car than its value. If the loss were settled on a fair market value, the insured might get more or less than the actual cash value of the car.

13. A: Errors and Omissions are also commonly known as E&O policies. This is a type of professional liability insurance that protects people who work in professions that offer professional advice to their clients or perform professional services. Typical professions include doctors, lawyers, insurance agents, consultants, and brokers. E & O insurance covers professionals from bearing the full cost of defending a civil lawsuit where the client alleges negligence due to an error or omission. With regard to insurance, it includes failing to insure with adequate limits or failing to explain pertinent conditions or exclusions of coverage.

14. D: A refrigerator is the personal property of the homeowner, so it could not be considered commercial property or inland marine property. As personal property of the homeowner, it is covered under the homeowner policy under Coverage C, personal property. It is covered anywhere in the world, even when it is being transported. The personal auto policy does not cover the insured's personal property that is not part of the automobile.

15. D: The HO-6 homeowner form covers the parts of the building that are not covered by a homeowner or property owner association. The HO-6 property form covers improvements and betterments that the insured installs such as in a condominium complex. It also covers the insured's personal property, liability, and medical payments.

16. C: The amount of required insurance is calculated by taking $200,000 times 80%, which equals $160,000. Since the insured only insured the home for $150,000, $150,000 would be divided by $160,000 to get a penalty of .9375. The $10,000 loss would be multiplied times the .9375 penalty to get $9375. The $1000 deductible would be subtracted to get $8375—the amount that would be payable to the insured as a final settlement.

17. C: The garage is covered under the homeowner's policy under Coverage B, other structures. Coverage B automatically covers 10% of Coverage A, the building coverage. If the $35,000 was not enough to replace it, the homeowner would have to pay the rest out of pocket or rebuild a less expensive garage. To prevent this problem, the homeowner could have increased the limit of coverage B to an amount that it would cost to rebuild the three-car garage.

18. B: A licensed property and casualty agent may sell the following:

- Home insurance
- Auto insurance
- Commercial property insurance
- Commercial liability insurance
- Casualty insurance
- Business owner's insurance

A property and casualty agent is not properly licensed to sell the following:

- Health insurance
- Life insurance
- Disability insurance
- Financial products.

19. B: A commercial package policy (CPP) consists of two or more of the following: buildings and personal property, business autos, commercial general liability, commercial crime, commercial inland marine, farm, employment practices liability, professional liability, boiler and machinery, and personal and advertising injury liability. Umbrella liability policies are sold as separate policies.

20. A: Dwellings must have four or fewer family units and be used exclusively as a residence. Thus, a mobile home, single-family home, and four-unit townhome would all qualify as a dwelling. Farms are not eligible for dwelling policies and must be insured under a farm owner policy.

21. B: When an insurer commonly accepts a practice, such as regularly accepting late payments, the insured expects that practice will continue to be accepted. Estoppel is a term that prevents the insurer from changing that position if accepting the late payments would result in causing harm to the insured. In this case, the harm would be that late payments could cause cancellation of the policy. A waiver is an intentional or voluntary relinquishment of some right, interest, etc. For example, an insured's deductible is waived if she incurs a total loss of her dwelling, meaning the insured does not have to pay the deductible. Fraud is an illegal act. Insurable interest is when the insured has a financial or legal interest in the property being insured.

22. D: An insurance contract is a legal contract between two parties. An insurance contract has five parts including the offer, consideration, acceptance, legal competence, and legal purpose. Insurance policies are not warranties, nor do they include any warranty coverage.

23. C: When several factors contribute to the cause of a loss, the peril that had the most significant impact on the resulting loss is called the proximate cause or direct cause. A remote cause can contribute to the loss, but it is not the proximate or direct cause. Probability of loss is a mathematical calculation, taking into account several types of information that estimates the probability that a loss will occur. An occurrence is an event.

24. C: Reinsurance is also known as insurance for insurers, or stop-loss insurance. Using actuarial data, insurers can predict how much they are likely to pay out in the event of a loss. The insurer sets a maximum amount of risk that they can pay out without risk of insolvency, which is also known as the retention limit. In the event of a loss, the insurer will pay the amount of the retention limit and cede any remaining amounts to the reinsurer. Reinsurance protects insurers from catastrophic-type losses.

25. A: A new homeowner would most likely purchase either an HO2 broad form, which is a named-perils policy, meaning if a peril is not specifically listed then it is not covered, or an HO3, which is an all-perils policy, meaning if a peril is not specifically excluded, then it is covered. An H01 is a basic, specified-only perils form and would not likely be purchased by a new homeowner as it would not provide broad enough coverage. HO4 is for tenants to insure their contents and provide liability on a broad, named-perils basis. HO5 is for tenants to insure their contents and provide liability on an all-perils basis. HO6 is for owners of condominiums.

26. B: The DP-3 covers open perils for the building damage. A DP-1 and DP-2 would also cover loss due to fire on a building. Since the landlord has added contents coverage on a DP-3 form, his contents are covered on an actual cash value basis up to the limit stated on the declarations.

27. C: Surplus lines brokers are licensed and permitted to place insurance with non-admitted insurers. Non-admitted insurers will insure risks that other insurers can't or won't insure. The insured accepts a larger degree of risk in using a surplus lines broker who insures her property with a non-admitted insurer because a non-admitted insurer is not required to follow state laws. The other options are not valid responses.

28. A: A maintenance bond guarantees the work after it has been completed. A bid bond guarantees the contract will be signed and the work completed. A performance bond guarantees the work will be completed. A payment bond guarantees all workers and subcontractors will be paid.

29. A: A commercial package policy covering business personal property will cover the buildings, business personal property, and liability. Land is always excluded under property policies, regardless of the cause of loss.

30. D: Water that saturates the land and is standing on top of the land is considered flooding. Flooding is not covered under a homeowner policy. Flood insurance can be purchased from FEMA. If the water damage was not due to flooding and the homeowner added a water back-up endorsement to her policy, there may have been some insurance coverage for the water damage.

31. B: Misrepresentation refers to false statements that are made by an insured that would have an effect on the insurer's decision to accept the risk or under what conditions to accept it. The misrepresentation in this case would give the insurer the right to cancel the policy. Fraud is when an insured commits an illegal act that leads to a financial loss to the insurer. Concealment is when an insured neglects to provide pertinent information. In this case, the insured concealed the fact that he had prior claims by lying, making it misrepresentation. Rebating is the process by which an insurance company return unearned premiums to an insured.

32. D: Coverage D is loss of use. It provides coverage for any extra expenses that an insured incurs because of not being able to occupy the home. This includes payment to stay in a hotel or rent another dwelling and extra costs for meals if the insured needs to dine out. Coverage A provides coverage for the dwelling. Coverage B provides coverage for other structures. Coverage C provides coverage for personal property.

33. C: A tort claim is filed by a third party who was injured or sustained damage by an insured party. The third party is entitled to reasonable monies to compensate for the loss, even when the injury is unintentional as it was in this case.

34. D: A claim that is made during the policy period is considered an occurrence, and the policy coverage is triggered by the date the event happened, when it happens during the policy period. A claims-made trigger extends coverage for the policy for a designated period of time, or "tail," after the policy period ends.

35. A: Freezing is an excluded peril under a business owner policy, so the insurer would pay nothing for this loss. The business owner would be liable for the pipe repair, the flooring, and the wall repair.

36. C: The declarations page includes basic information about the policy, including the named parties, the type of property, the eligible insured locations, policy period, coverage limits, and deductibles. The policy definitions, conditions, and exclusions would be outlined in the policy.

37. B: The insurer has 30 days to pay for a loss once they have received proof of the loss. Proof of loss could be in the form of receipts, bills, photographs, personal inspection, or other proof of the loss.

38. D: There are three parties to a surety bond. The first party is the surety, who guarantees the performance of the second party, or the principal. The performance of the principal is guaranteed to the third party, the obligee.

39. B: Newly-acquired and constructed buildings will be covered for a maximum of $250,000 for the building and $100,000 for business personal property when the building or property is acquired during the policy term. Coverage lasts for up to 30 days of the acquisition of the property or 30 days from the time construction begins, unless the policy expires prior to that time. The extension also expires when the insured reports actual values to the insurer.

40. B: Although all of the bonds in the answers are actual types of bonds, only performance, surety, bid, and maintenance bonds are all three-party bonds that would often be purchased by contractors.

Property Insurance Terms and Related Concepts

Duties of an Insurance Agent

An **insurance agent** acts as a representative of an insurance company. Insurance agents must be detail oriented (insurance policies contain a lot of information), have exceptional "people" skills (dealing with people on a daily basis is an integral part of their career), be excellent communicators (they have to be able to explain what they are selling), and be able to close sales (selling insurance policies is how insurance agents make their living).

Insurance agents have two distinct roles and several responsibilities. First, insurance agents sell insurance policies issued by the insurance company. Insurance companies compensate insurance agents, meaning agents get paid to sell policies on behalf of the company. This compensation is commonly referred to as **commission**. Depending on their employment contract, insurance agents may earn a salary, a commission on sales, or a combination of both. Second, an insurance agent services insurance policies issued by the insurance companies to clients.

Some of the duties performed by insurance agents are discussed next.

Policy Sales

Insurance agents sell insurance policies to clients. **Policy sales** generate premiums for the insurance company and commission for the insurance agent.

Prospecting

A prospect is a person or business that has an interest or need to buy a product or service offered. **Prospecting** is the practice of actively seeking these interested parties and asking them to consider a product that meets their needs, in this case, an insurance policy. Insurance agents must be constantly generating new prospects, as this is usually how their compensation is determined.

Providing Quotes

An insurance **quote** provides the projected cost of covering a defined risk. Insurance quotes are not offers of insurance. Quotes are generated by gathering information about the risk and providing a quote, or price, based on the insurance company's rates. For example, an initial quote for property insurance could be based on facts such as the type of construction of the dwelling (wood, brick, or some other material) and how close the home is to a fire hydrant. Further information would be needed before a final quote is offered (e.g., if the area is prone to flooding). Final quotes are generated by the field underwriting division of an insurance company.

Field Underwriting

Insurance companies assess risk exposure as it pertains to issuing policies, which is how premiums are calculated. As such, policies that expose the insurance company to greater risks charge more premiums than lower risk policies. As an agent representing the insurance company, your responsibility is to identify risks, charge appropriate premiums, or, in some cases, refuse the coverage altogether. Insurance companies depend on their insurance agents to identify discrepancies, inconsistencies, and cases of outright fraud in order to limit their liability. Insurance agents are **field underwriters**, that is they are "in the field" or close to where the risks are. Insurance companies also have an underwriting department that determines what premiums to charge using various calculation methods.

Policy Delivery, Countersigning, and Binding Authority

Any policy that has been issued by a company must be **delivered** to the insured. An agent must review the policy to make sure it meets the coverage applied for and the appropriate premium is being charged. Once the agent has reviewed the policy and delivered it to the client, both the client and the agent will sign the policy. Though it is customary for both the agent and the insured to **countersign** the policy, the coverage is actually in force from the date stated in the insurance policy application.

In many cases, insurance agents will have **binding authority** absent of a written contract. For example, an insurance agent, when authorized to do so, could provide a client with coverage for the house they just purchased until the client can meet with the insurance agent to sign the policy. Binding insurance coverage in this way would generally be done over the phone.

Service

While a policy is in force, insurance agents are responsible for making changes, or **servicing**, the policy at the client's request. Examples of possible changes include the insured purchasing an additional property or moving to a new address. Insurance agents also may report any claims to the insurance company. Finally, when an insurance policy is renewed, insurance agents need to discuss any changes, such as an increase in premiums, with their clients.

Other Insurance Professionals

Insurance agents regularly interact with other **insurance professionals**. What follows are some examples of positions others hold within the insurance industry.

Consultants

Insurance consumers, your potential clients, may hire **consultants** who aid them in purchasing insurance products. Consultants provide advice on which policies are needed and recommend coverage. Insurance agents may be contacted by consultants asking for a quote on their client's behalf.

In the event that an insurance agent is contacted by a **consultant**, or anyone else, concerning an existing policy, they must be diligent when it comes to following privacy laws. It is important that insurance agents never discuss existing policies with anyone other than the insured unless they have permission from the insured to do so. There are both federal and state rules in place in regard to privacy.

Solicitors

Under the direction of a licensed insurance agent, **solicitors** can recruit clients and provide quotes. Because solicitors are not licensed to sell insurance, they cannot countersign policies, nor do they have any binding authority.

Brokers

Instead of being an insurance agent working for one insurance company, **brokers** represent different insurance companies. Brokers compare the coverage needed in addition to the premiums charged by the insurance companies they represent in order to find the most appropriate policy for their clients.

For example, if Johnny works for ABC Insurance Company, then he can only sell policies issued by ABC Insurance Company. If Johnny works for 123 Insurance Brokerage, Johnny can sell insurance policies issued by ABC Insurance Company, DEF Insurance Company, and GHI Insurance Company.

Excess/Surplus Lines

Clients sometimes require coverage for non-standard risks. When this type of insurance coverage is needed, **excess** or **surplus lines** provide the coverage. Excess or surplus is defined as "additional," which is a way to remember what kind of coverage these insurance policies provide. Examples include policies that cover damage to the hands of a professional pianist, professional athletes who cover damage to their bodies, and singers who cover damage to their voices.

Producers

All of the above-mentioned professionals, as well as agents, are considered to be **producers**. A person who provides insurance in return for commissions (agents), fees (consultants), or other compensation are said to be "producing" insurance policies.

Agency Relationship

Understanding the **agency relationship** is important because it is an integral part of doing business in the insurance industry. An agency relationship clearly defines the responsibilities of the insurance company and the insurance agent. Because insurance companies provide insurance to clients in a wide geographical area, they employ insurance agents to sell policies on their behalf. Maintaining a healthy and cooperative agency relationship is imperative to doing business.

An example of a situation similar to the agency relationship is the relationship between a school principal and the teachers in the school. Part of a principal's job is to enforce school rules, but the principal cannot be everywhere at once. Principals employ teachers to act on their behalf when it comes to enforcing the school rules. If a student were late getting to class without a valid reason, the teacher may give the student a detention, which is the rule to be followed, as set out by the principal, in disciplining a student who is late.

Just as teachers attend staff meetings and professional development days in order to stay current on the school rules, most states require a set number of hours of continuing education in order for insurance agents to have their licenses renewed.

Property and Casualty Insurance

Property and casualty are the two major classifications of insurance. **Property insurance** provides money to repair or replace the physical property of an insured and the revenue they may earn from that property in the event that a legitimate claim has been reported. **Casualty insurance**, also referred to as **liability insurance**, provides money should an insured "cause" damage or loss to another party. Casualty insurance can also protect an insured from a loss caused by another party that does not have the means or insurance protection to financially restore the damaged caused.

Classifications

Insurance companies that offer only one type of insurance are known as **mono-line** insurers. For example, they sell only property insurance. Insurance companies that offer more than one type of insurance are known as **multi-line** insurers. For example, they sell property and automobile insurance. Insurance companies may sell policies just to individuals (**personal lines**) or just to businesses (**commercial lines**), or they may sell to both parties. Personal line and commercial line policies cover both property and casualty (liability) coverage, and both types of policies cover losses incurred by legitimate claims. As their names imply, personal line policies cover property owned by individuals, while commercial line policies cover property owned by businesses.

Perils and Hazards

A **peril** is defined as any occurrence that causes a loss. For example, if a grease fire destroys a kitchen, the peril is the fire. If strong winds cause damage to a roof, the wind is the peril. A **hazard** is anything that increases the probability that there will be a loss. Consider a large oak tree that has rotted in the backyard of a house. If the tree is not cut down, it is creating a hazard because it is likely to fall over at some point and could fall on the house, causing damage.

Three types of hazards are physical, moral, and morale. A **physical hazard** refers to the condition of the actual property, including how it is used, what state of repair it is in, and whether there are people present to damage the property, or experience harm because of the condition of the property. An abandoned home with no locks and an uncovered pool with no fence are examples of physical hazards, as anyone could easily enter the home and vandalize it, or a child could fall into the pool and drown.

A **moral hazard** occurs when an insured does something that intentionally causes a loss to occur and the insured will profit from the loss. Actions of moral hazard are fraudulent in nature. For example, an insured is behind on their mortgage payments. In order to collect insurance money, instead of letting their house go into foreclosure, the insured sets the house on fire. The cause of the loss was intended by the insured, as opposed to being unintentional. The insured is committing fraud.

Morale hazard constitutes a person's behavior and therefore cannot be "seen" by the insurance company when assessing the risk. A morale hazard is defined as the attitude of the insured. They may be indifferent about their behavior, for instance, which can lead to a loss. It is difficult for insurance companies to assess morale hazard because it pertains to the way a person thinks; morale hazards are attitudes as opposed to actions. In addition, they are unintended, meaning the insured is not trying to cause a loss to occur, they are just careless in their thinking.

To illustrate, an insured resides in an area where there is a lot of vandalism and burglaries, which lead to property damage. The insured does not install perimeter lighting around the outside of their house nor do they install deadbolt locks or an alarm system, which are all actions that could reduce the chance that a loss would occur. The insured is not intentionally doing anything that would cause a loss, but they are not doing anything to reduce the probability of a loss.

When remembering how to distinguish between *moral* and *morale* hazards, think of moral as being something that happens on purpose and morale as something that is an unintended.

Direct Loss and Indirect Loss

A **direct loss,** also referred to as a consequential loss, is a loss of property or property value caused by a peril. An **indirect loss** is the additional costs the insured incurs as a result of the covered direct loss event. A house fire is a direct loss, while the additional cost the homeowner pays to stay in a hotel while the house is being repaired is an indirect or consequential loss.

It is important to know that not all policies extend indirect loss coverage as part of the base policy. In regard to the aforementioned house fire, the insurance policy may cover the damage caused by the fire but might not pay the hotel bill incurred by the homeowner.

Calculating the Reimbursement Value of a Property Insurance Policy

When paying a claim, insurance companies have various methods and calculations they use to determine how the claim will be paid.

These are the options available to insurance companies when paying claims:

- **Actual cash value (AVC)** is the cost of the item less depreciation. For example, if a five-year-old television is destroyed by fire, the insurance company would pay what the television was worth at the time of the loss. The television may have cost $1,000 three years ago but the value of the television has depreciated, or lessened, since it was purchased, and it is now only worth $200. When paying for the television based on actual cash value, the insurance company would pay $200.

- **Repair cost** refers to the stated cost to repair a damaged item. For example, if a laptop is damaged, but not destroyed, the insurance company would pay to have the laptop repaired.

- **Replacement cost** is similar to actual cash value except depreciation is not deducted from the value. This option is more expensive for the insured to purchase. For example, if a five-year-old refrigerator is destroyed by fire, the insurance company would replace the refrigerator with a new model that is as similar as possible to the one that was lost.

- **Functional replacement cost** is similar to repair cost but with less expensive material. Suppose a window was broken. The insurance company may be able to find a replacement window that is not new but would adequately replace the broken window.

- **Market value** is what the item is worth at the time of loss. A gold ring purchased fifteen years ago may be worth much more today if the price of gold has increased substantially. This method of calculating value can leave much to interpretation, which can lead to disputes between the insurance company and the insured.

- **Valuation condition** is the value of the property at the time the loss occurred. Policy wordings will state how the value of the property is to be calculated if a loss occurs. Usually, the insurance company will retain the right to pay any claims based on the lowest calculated value.

- **Co-insurance condition**, also referred to as a **deductible**, is the amount that the insured is required to pay toward any claim. In essence, both the insurance company and the insured are responsible for paying any losses and the co-insurance condition, or deductible, simply states the amount or percentage each party is responsible for. An example of this is a property policy with a $2,000 deductible. If there is a loss that is determined by the valuation condition in the policy to be less than $2,000, the insured is solely responsible for the repair or replacement. However, if the damage is determined to be $10,000, the insured would be responsible for $2,000 and the insurance company would be responsible for $8,000. The co-insurance condition, or deductible, is stated in the declarations section of the insurance policy. In some instances, where a total loss is incurred, insurance companies may waive, or not charge, the deductible.

- **Proximate cause** is similar to an indirect loss in that a claim would not have otherwise occurred if a base event did not happen. If an additional loss can be traced back to a base event such as fire or weather, without an interruption or intervening cause, the loss occurred due to proximate cause. An **intervening cause** is a separate event that causes a loss. As an example, wind from a thunderstorm rips the roof off a store, and rainwater damages the contents. The contents were not damaged by wind; however, if the wind did not blow off the roof, the contents would not have been damaged. This defines proximate cause. If the same store were damaged by a fire, but a thunderstorm comes the next day and causes additional damage to the building and contents, the thunderstorm would be considered an intervening cause.

Insurance Company Divisions

Administration

Executives of an insurance company, such as the president, work in the **administration** department.

Underwriting/Actuaries

Policies are reviewed, checked for accuracy and rated by the **underwriting** department. Insurance rates are determined by analyzing historical data obtained from many sources. Statistical data is one type of information used when determining what risks the insurance company wants to cover and what premium they should charge. For example, an insurance company may look at the number of tornadoes that caused damage in a specific geographical region over the past 10 years.

Actuaries are responsible for gathering and analyzing data in order to help decide how much insurance companies should charge for their policies. If an area experiences frequent tornadoes, for example, insurance companies may charge a higher premium for damage caused by a tornado, or they may exclude damage caused by a tornado all together.

Investments

An insurance company's assets must be carefully invested. The assets invested must be predictably liquid. At any given time, large amounts of claims could occur, and the company may find it necessary to liquidate a portion of their **investments** in order to honor claims. Earning interest is an important factor, as all insurance companies like to make a profit, but liquidity and predictability are most important when investment options are chosen.

Claims

When a loss is incurred, it is reported to the **claims** department to determine merit and accuracy.

Claim adjusters are an integral part of the process, as they inspect the damage and provide information about the cost of repairs or replacement. Some insurance companies employ their own claim adjusters while others hire them as independent contractors.

Accounting

Insurance companies handle large amounts of money. Their main source of income is policy premiums. The **accounting** department is responsible for issuing commissions, salaries, premium credits, claims payments, capital reserves, and any other financial transactions. Insurance companies are subject to strict regulation and must submit statements of financial condition to the Commissioner's offices in the states where they are writing insurance. Accurate accounting is incredibly important to the insurance process.

Distribution, Marketing, Auditing, and Legal

Distribution is the department responsible for policy sales. Companies employ insurance agents, independent brokers, or a combination of both. The distribution department recruits insurance agents and trains them on the products offered.

Marketing is a key component of distribution. Companies tend to focus on particular areas of insurance that favor profitability. The marketing department develops strategies to notify, educate, and ultimately gain the business of target markets using, for example, television and Internet ads, billboard signage, and direct postal mail.

Auditing is the practice of determining the difference in premium an insured paid compared with the risk that was actually in place. Risks, such as those incurred with workers' compensation and general liability policies, are subject to change and are reviewed by auditing departments on a regular basis, usually once a year on the policy renewal date. Holders of such policies, the insureds, may be required to submit payroll statements, receipts of various natures, employee censuses, and accounting records to the insurance company. Audit departments review the information provided by the insured and determine if the premium being charged is sufficient. **Loss control** is a proactive method of educating policyholders on risk reduction measures that can be taken to avoid loss. These measures are required before policies are offered. If, for instance, there are no steps leading to an exterior door, which could cause injury if someone opened the door and fell, the insurance company may require that the steps be installed prior to offering coverage.

Legal

An insurance policy is a legal contract, and disputes about the contract do arise. **Legal** departments are responsible for keeping the insurance company in compliance with laws and regulations. It is also responsible for defending the company in legal disputes.

Loss Control

Insurance companies do not usually take full financial responsibility for all risks they insure. There are limits to the amount of risk they can retain without compromising their reserve requirements.

Reinsurance is simply insurance for insurance companies. The reinsurance department is responsible for acquiring policies from a reinsurer and making sure the company stays within the parameters agreed to with the reinsurance company.

Policy Limits of Liability Insurance

The maximum amount an insurance company will pay for a loss is known as the **policy limit.** This limit is stated in the declarations part of the insurance policy. Below are some of the limit descriptions found in common liability policies.

- **Per occurrence/per accident limit** is the total amount the insurance company will pay on a single loss per incident no matter how much property is damaged nor how many people are affected. For example, a house burns down, and several people are injured. The per occurrence/per accident limit is the total amount the insurance company will pay to repair/replace the house along with covering the injuries.

- **Per person limit** is the total amount the insurance company will pay to any one person per claim. Suppose a person is injured when they fall in a hole located on the insured's property. This is the total amount the insurance company will pay that person for their injuries.

- **Aggregate limit** is the total amount the insurance company will pay no matter how many claims there are over the course of the policy period, most commonly one year. For example, an insured has five claims over the course of their policy period. This is the total amount the insurance company will pay, which could result in only four of the claims being covered because the full aggregate limit was used up to satisfy payment for the first four claims. Therefore, the fifth claim would not be paid.

- **Voluntary liability limit** is the total amount the insurance company may choose to pay per liability claim without admitting that it is actually liable for the damage. This limit is commonly used when the cost to legally defend a claim is likely to be higher than just paying the claim without going through legal procedures such as going to court. For example, a person slips on ice and a claim is filed for their injuries. If the insurance company can settle with the injured person for $2,500 without admitting that it was the insured's fault because they failed to clear the ice from their walkway, it may choose to pay the claim as prolonging the claim would incur much more than $2,500 in expenses.

Regulation

Insurance companies and the policies they offer are regulated by individual states and their respective Commissioners. In addition, there are federal regulations. Insurance companies come under three categories. **Domestic** insurers do business in their home state. **Foreign** insurers do business in other states as well as in their home state. **Alien** insurers do business in another country.

Once an insurance company has satisfied the state's regulations, the state Commissioner will recognize the insurance company as an **admitted** insurer. Occasionally, an insurance company may not meet all of the state's regulations, but the Commissioner will still grant it permission to sell insurance in that state. The insurance company is then referred to as a **non-admitted** insurer.

The state Commissioner is also responsible for regulating insurance agents. Insurance agents have specific requirements that must be met to obtain and keep a license to sell insurance. Listed below are some of the key requirements a state may require.

Licensing

Insurance agents must be **licensed** by the state before they can sell insurance. An exam must be taken and passed in order to obtain a license. Insurance agents may also be required to take various courses, as defined by the state regulations, in order to renew their license each year.

Fiduciary Responsibility

Insurance agents collect premiums and may also deliver claim payments to an insured. Because this constitutes a **fiduciary responsibility**, insurance agents may have to disclose personal financial information to the Commissioner.

Prohibited Practices

Insurance is a closely regulated industry. Insurance agents must not participate in or execute **prohibited practices**. Doing so may lead to their license being suspended or revoked and could result in criminal charges.

- **Twisting:** When an insurance agent convinces an insured to cancel their existing policy and open a new policy, and the transaction costs the insured more money while benefitting the insurance agent financially, perhaps in the form of additional commission or bonuses being paid, this is called **twisting.** For example, an insurance broker, who sells insurance for several different insurance companies, sells a property policy to a client that is due to be in force for one year, and the insured pays for the policy. The insurance broker gets paid a commission as compensation for writing the new policy. Two months later, the insurance broker convinces that same client to cancel their property insurance, and the insurance broker issues them another policy through a different insurer that may be more expensive but provides the same coverage. The broker then receives compensation in the form of commission again. This transaction ultimately costs the insured more money, because they cancelled their policy early and the new policy cost them more money for less coverage. In addition, the insurance broker received commission twice when, if they had left the original policy in force, they would only have received commission once.

- **False advertising:** When insurance agents misrepresent, or omit pertinent information about, a company or policy, clients are unable to make an informed decision. This constitutes **false advertising**, which is unethical and a prohibited practice.

- **Rebating:** When an agent offers a financial incentive to a client to purchase a policy, like paying a non-licensed client a portion of their commission, this is referred to as **rebating**. For example, if an insurance agent tells an insured that they will pay them $50 cash out of their commission if the insured purchases a property policy, this prohibited process is called rebating.

Policy Rate (Premium) Determination Methods

Not all risks to be insured fall under normal criteria. When enough statistical data is not available to determine a rate, other measures are used to calculate premiums.

- **Merit rating** is a process by which a base rate is set, with the flexibility to adjust the rate based on additional factors. The major factor used to determine the rate adjustment is loss experience. **Loss experience** is the examination of loss claims by an insured over a period of time. The more losses claimed, the higher the adjustment for premium.

- **Schedule rating** is a credit/debit system, where an insurance company will examine different attributes of a company. Factors such as years in operation, experience of the principal and key employees, and loss potential are some of the criteria used to determine the premium.

- **Retrospective rating** is the practice of adjusting premiums based on changes in risks and losses claimed during the current coverage period. The insured pays a base premium, and, if anything occurs that increases risk, or a loss occurs, the premium will be increased accordingly. Workers' compensation policies employ this kind of rating. An employer does not know how many people they will hire or fire in a year, so premiums are adjusted at the end of the policy period to reflect the actual number of employees that were covered under the policy.

Application Process for Acquiring Insurance and Binders

All insurance contracts begin with an **application** for coverage. An application contains specific questions that must be answered accurately and honestly by the applicant. Sometimes the answers given will lead to further questions from underwriters. Agents are responsible for checking the application's accuracy and submitting it to the insurance company (also known as the carrier).

If the agent has the express authority to bind the insurance company to the coverage offered, they can bind the coverage while the insurance company reviews the information and creates a policy. A **binder** creates immediate insurance coverage on the written or verbal word of the agent. It is important to note that a binder does not obligate the insurer to issue a policy, it only obligates the insurer to pay a claim should one arise while the underwriting process is being completed. Binders are often used when an insured needs coverage outside of normal office hours.

Federal and State Regulation of Insurance Companies

Insurance regulations are primarily administered through state Commissioners; however, there are a few Federal regulations that are applicable to insurers and the policies they issue.

- The **Fair Credit Reporting Act** is applicable because credit scores are often used to determine coverage eligibility and rates.
- The **Federal Emergency Management Agency (FEMA)** and the **National Flood Insurance Program** are federal agencies that usually deal with natural disasters on a national level; therefore, federal regulations are necessary to have continuity across all states suffering disasters.
- The top insurance regulator for a state is the **Commissioner.** This is usually an elected position, and the Commissioner is responsible for regulating insurance activity in their state. Commissioners ensure that insurance agents, as well as the insurance companies they sell policies for, are following the consumer protection measures put in place by the state.
- The **National Association of Insurance Commissioners (NAIC)** comprises all the state Commissioners. The association meets to discuss developments in their respective states and across the country.

Specific Insurance and Blanket Insurance

An insurance policy is a legal contract. A contract is a binding agreement between consenting parties. The agreement must specify what is agreed to within the contract, which is covered in the **declarations** section of a policy. When an insurance contract states what is covered and for what amount, these are the **specifics** of the insurance policy. A typical homeowners' policy may have contents coverage, which is in place to provide coverage for the contents in the home should they be damaged or destroyed by an insured peril. Though it is a good practice to inventory the items within a house, in regard to household contents coverage, insurance policies are designed to cover the usual contents that would be in an average home. If an insured has contents that would be considered over and above what is in an average home, such as a full grand piano, they can sometimes purchase additional coverage for these items for an additional premium.

A policy that extends the same specific coverage over multiple properties is a **blanket insurance** policy. Blanket insurance does not mean that everything is covered for any kind of loss, as some may think the term implies. There are no insurance policies that provide coverage for anything that could possibly happen. All insurance policies will have exclusions.

Endorsements

The **endorsement** section of an insurance policy is where coverage, terms, or changes to the insurance policy wording are listed. These changes are also referred to as **riders.** For example, if coverage for sewer backup is not included in the usual property insurance wording, the insured may elect to purchase optional coverage for sewer backup losses, which may be available for an additional premium. This change would be listed in the endorsement section.

Concurrent Causation

When two claim events occur at the same time, resulting in two claims against the same policy, this is referred to as **concurrent causation**. Claims paid as a result of concurrent causation have been the subject of much confusion and litigation, because one event often causes the other event to occur. Sometimes a policy may appear to have conflicting coverages, or the lack thereof. For example, a policy may cover damage to a business sign, but it may not cover roof damage from a named tropical storm or hurricane. If an insured's business sign is blown onto their roof and causes both the sign and roof to be damaged, all during a named hurricane, there could be some confusion as to what caused the claim, and what should be paid. Insurance companies include specific language regarding coverage and exclusions, but every possible scenario cannot be listed which can lead to disputes between the parties.

Co-Insurance Condition and Co-Insurance Penalty

An insurance policy outlines the co-insurance conditions and penalties. A **co-insurance condition** states that an insured can only receive the maximum claim limit if they have purchased a policy covering a specified minimum amount. Co-insurance conditions are usually expressed as a percentage but can be a stated amount or agreed amount, expressed as a dollar value. A policy with a co-insurance condition will only insure the percentage of the loss that is stated in the contract. If a property is valued at $100,000, and the owner chooses to insure it for $50,000, or fifty percent of the value, the insurance company will only pay fifty percent of any claims that occur. If there is a claim filed and the amount of the loss is determined to be $10,000, the insured will receive $5,000, which is fifty percent of the claim. The $5,000 that is not covered would be the responsibility of the insured and is called the **co-insurance penalty.**

Pair or Set Condition

Property comprising more than one part is insured under a **pair or set condition.** The individual parts are usually worth less on their own than as part of the pair or set and if one of the individual components is damaged or lost, the overall value of the pair or set is also diminished. For example, if a pair of shoes cost $2,000, the shoes are worth $2,000 as a pair or set, but if one shoe is lost, the remaining shoe may only be worth $200. If the owner insured the shoes, and lost one of them, the insurance company would have to pay a claim for the difference between the value of the pair less the value of the one shoe, which would equate to an $1,800 payment ($2,000 value of shoes – $200 value of one shoe = $1,800).

Salvage Condition and Abandonment Condition

Within an insurance contract there are rights an insurance company has and obligations the insured has. **Salvage conditions** are the rights a company has to pay replacement cost and take ownership of the property. This would allow the company to sell the property if desired and reduce the total expenses resulting from the claim. For example, if there was damage to a shed, the insurance company could choose to replace the shed with a new one and sell the damaged shed in order to recoup some of their loss associated with the claim.

Abandonment conditions also protect the company, but it places a requirement on the insured.

Under the abandonment condition, an insured must not leave the property unattended because this increases the possibility of a claim and could reduce the value of the property. If a homeowner is away for an extended period of time, for example, and leaves their home unattended, there is a greater likelihood the home could be vandalized, which could reduce the value of the home.

Arbitration Condition and Appraisal Condition

Arbitration conditions are common in all contractual agreements, and they are simply a description of how disputes will be decided. The process described should be understood by all parties before entering into the contract. An **appraisal condition** is a form of arbitration that outlines what courses of action the insured and insurer have in the event of a dispute of value. For example, an insured and insurer may have the right to hire an independent adjuster to determine the value of the damage in question. If the parties are still unable to agree, the insured and insurer could split the cost of a third adjuster to render their opinion. If two of the three adjusters agree on an amount, then that will be the amount paid regardless of whether the parties still disagree.

Other Insurance Condition and Coverages

- **Other insurance condition** applies when a property is insured by multiple policies. It prevents moral hazards, in that a property owner can't be incentivized to experience loss. The condition explains how the multiple policies will coordinate and to what extent.
- **Primary** and **excess coverage** describes when there are two companies insuring the same property; one will be named **primary** and the other will be named as **excess**. This means that the primary insurer will pay first, and up to the limit of their policy, before the excess insurer will begin their payment. For example, if a building were valued at $10,000,000, the primary insurer may provide $8,000,000 coverage, and the excess insurer would provide $2,000,000.
- **Pro-rated** or **pro-rata coverage** is similar to primary and excess coverage. It also involves multiple policies insuring the same property. The difference is the participation rate. In **pro-rated** or **pro-rata coverage**, the insurers participate in the claim payment in accordance to the percentage they insure the property. Insurance Company One may have 60% of the coverage, and Insurance Company Two would then have 40%. If a claim arises, Company One will pay 60% of the claim, and Company Two will pay 40% of the claim.
- **Concurrent** coverage means that multiple insurance policies cover the same risks. **Non-concurrent** coverage also involves multiple insurance policies covering the same risks; however, there are differences in the policies. The wordings of the insurance policies are different, and the covered and excluded perils along with any endorsements may differ as well. Non-concurrent policies are the basis of much litigation and are usually avoided.

Liberalization Condition, Assignment Condition, and No Benefit to Bailee Condition

Liberalization condition is the right of the insurer to broaden coverage on an entire class of similar policies without a new endorsement being issued to all in-force policies. The coverage cannot result in an increase in premium nor can it result in a decrease in coverage for the insured during the existing policy period. For example, if an insurance company changes their property insurance policies to cover losses caused by all chimney fires, even if the chimney is not in compliance with new building codes, all existing property policies will automatically be covered by those losses. However, the insurance company cannot charge existing policy holders an extra premium for the coverage until the policy is renewed.

An **assignment condition** is when the rights and benefits of a contract are transferred to another party. Policies are not transferrable unless the original policy owner dies or provides written permission granting authority. For example, if a policy owner dies, the person(s) designated as the beneficiary of their property would then become the owner of the policy.

Assignment condition is a common practice when dealing with mortgaged properties. When a policy owner dies, there is a **transfer of rights** that allows their successor to maintain the policy and file claims. Consider that if a policy owner dies, the mortgagee has an interest in their property because it is being used as collateral for a loan. As such, the mortgagee would be able to make changes to the policy, such as asking for a vacancy permit to be issued.

The **no benefit to bailee condition** prevents a party other than the insured from collecting any claim payment while in temporary possession of the insured property. The owner of the policy is the only party entitled to benefit. For example, a homeowner has a friend housesitting for them while they are on vacation. During the time they are away, there is a broken pipe that causes damage. The housesitting friend cannot receive payment in their name from the insurance company for the damage.

Mortgage and Policy Territory Conditions and Vacancy and Unoccupancy Provisions

Mortgage condition is also referred to as a **loss payable condition.** The mortgage condition explains the rights a mortgage holder has and usually includes filing claims and paying premiums should the policy owner be unable to. This condition essentially allows a bank or mortgage company to make sure the property used as collateral for a loan is protected against loss.

The **policy territory condition** defines where coverage is extended. Most policies only cover property in the US, Canada, and Puerto Rico. Property transported outside the territory, or property owned in another country by the insured, would not be covered, unless specified in the declaration or endorsement section of their insurance policy.

Vacancy Provisions

It is well documented that vacant properties are at a greater risk for loss; therefore, policies contain **vacancy provisions.** This provision limits coverage when properties are left vacant and unattended. For example, if an insured goes on vacation for six weeks and does not have a responsible, designated person checking their home daily, and there is a flood in the house due to a broken pipe, the insurance company may reserve the right to not cover the claim. In addition, if an insured dies and their house is left vacant, the mortgagee may request that the insurance company issue a "vacancy permit." The permit, if approved, would be issued for a specific period of time and would list perils that are and are not covered. There may be coverage for fire but not for vandalism.

Coverage for water damage (including sprinklers), vandalism, theft, and glass breakage will cease after the building has been considered vacant for 60 consecutive days or more and other insured perils will only be eligible for 85% of the policy limits.

Glossary of Common Insurance Terms

Combined ratio is how the insurance company determines its profits and losses. If the losses and expenses exceed the premiums collected, this constitutes a loss. If the losses and expenses are less than the premiums collected, this equates to a profit.

Earned premium is the portion of the policy premium that has been used. For example, if an insurance policy is issued for a period of twelve months, at six months into the policy, half of the total premium has been earned.

Expense ratio is the practice of dividing an insurance company's expenses by the total amount of premium collected. Examples of expenses include agent commissions, employee salaries, adjuster's fees, and advertising costs.

Incurred losses are all expenses associated with losses and claims. Examples include loss payments to settle claims, appraisals, adjuster's fees, and legal expenses.

Loss ratio is calculated by dividing the incurred loss figure by the earned premium figure. It is a commonly used indicator of an insurance company's performance.

Underwriting expenses are all expenses associated with underwriting and issuing policies.

Agent commissions, corporate salaries, and costs to gather information that assists in determining premiums are examples of usual underwriting expenses.

Written premiums are an insurance company's sum of premiums from all sources.

Practice Questions

1. When a licensed insurance producer has an agency relationship with an insurer, which of the following acts are they not allowed to perform on behalf of the company?
   a. Bind coverage on behalf of the company
   b. Collect premiums for the company
   c. Decide what premiums to charge the insured
   d. Countersign insurance policies

2. A property owner never locks their doors or windows when they are not home, thus increasing the possibility that someone could easily enter their home and steal their belongings. This is an example of which type of hazard?
   a. Morale hazard
   b. Moral hazard
   c. Health hazard
   d. Physical hazard

3. The clause in an insurance contract/policy that reduces the amount of reimbursement to settle a claim due to the insured not purchasing enough insurance is known as:
   a. Valuation condition
   b. Proximate cause condition
   c. Co-insurance condition
   d. Salvage condition

4. A company that offers home and automobile insurance is BEST known as a:
   a. Multi-line insurer
   b. Mono-line insurer
   c. Personal line insurer
   d. Commercial line insurer

5. Which of the following departments would be responsible for setting premium rates for a workers' compensation policy after reviewing their payroll reports for the past year?
   a. Investment department
   b. Underwriting department
   c. Audit department
   d. Claims department

6. The maximum amount a company will pay for a loss that occurs at a specific time and place is BEST described as:
   a. Per occurrence/accident limit
   b. Voluntary liability limit
   c. Per person limit
   d. Aggregate limit

7. If an agent persuades a client to cancel and replace their current policy with a new one in order to earn commission or other compensation for themselves, this is known as:
   a. Rebating
   b. Twisting
   c. Merit rating
   d. Express authority

8. Repair cost is BEST described as:
   a. The amount necessary to replace a damaged item
   b. The amount necessary to repair a damaged item
   c. The replacement cost minus depreciation
   d. The amount necessary to repair a damaged item to functional ability with an after-market part.

9. A producer with an agency relationship can do all of the following EXCEPT:
   a. Bind coverage
   b. Collect premiums
   c. Determine claim amounts
   d. Assist with the claim process

10. Which term refers to items that are more valuable together than apart?
   a. Separate but equal
   b. Pair or set
   c. Multi line
   d. Actual cash value

11. A foreign company, when related to insurance companies, is best described as:
   a. An insurance company from another country
   b. An insurance company from another state
   c. An insurance company listed as a non-admitted carrier
   d. An insurance company operating as a co-insurer

12. The total amount of premium an insurer is due in a given period is referred to as:
   a. Earned premium
   b. Written premium
   c. Net premium
   d. Short-rate premium

13. Changes to a policy are listed in which section?
   a. Endorsements
   b. Conditions
   c. Declarations
   d. Assignments

14. The owner of ABC Company has left their insured store premises abandoned for three months, but they put a deadbolt lock on all of the doors and made sure the windows were locked. The insured has not been back to the premises in the three months, nor has the owner designated someone to check on his property. The property insurance policy for ABC Company does not expire for six months. Today, vandals break the windows and steal property that was left inside the store. How will ABC Company's insurance coverage be affected?

a. Due to the vacancy clause, the entire loss will be covered as the premises has not been abandoned for more than 180 days.

b. Due to the vacancy clause, the window damage will be covered but the theft of the items will not be covered.

c. Due to the vacancy clause, only 50% of the loss will be covered.

d. Due to the vacancy clause, there will be no coverages as the building has been vacant for more than 60 consecutive days.

Answer Explanations

1. C: A producer with an agency relationship is allowed to perform all of the acts listed except decide premiums. Premiums are decided by a company's underwriting department.

2. A: Morale hazard applies to loss due to careless or reckless behavior. Moral hazard applies to dishonest or illegal behavior. Physical hazard applies to actual property. Health hazard is not an applicable answer.

3. C: The co-insurance condition requires an insured to purchase a minimum amount of property insurance to receive the full reimbursement allowed by the contract in the event of a loss. Proximate cause applies to uninterrupted events leading to a secondary loss. Valuation condition applies to how the property is valued in order to determine the loss amount payable. Salvage condition gives the insurer the right to salvage and dispose of property (primarily by selling the property) in order to reduce their cost of paying a claim.

4. A: Multi-line insurers offer multiple lines of insurance. Mono-line insurers offer only one type of insurance. Personal lines deal with individuals. Commercial lines deal with companies or entities.

5. C: The audit department audits the payrolls of an insured to determine rates. Investment departments handle the investing of company's assets. Underwriting departments determine risk and the premiums associated with the risk to be insured. The claims department handles claims.

6. A: The per occurrence/accident limit is the maximum an insurance company will pay for a loss event that occurs at a specific time and place. The voluntary liability limit is the maximum amount the insurance company will pay without the company admitting to being liable. The per person limit is the maximum amount the insurance company will pay per each person involved in a claim. The aggregate limit is the maximum amount the insurance company will pay for all claims.

7. B: *C* and *D* are not applicable. Rebating is when an agent agrees to pay an unlicensed representative a portion of their commission.

8. B: The amount necessary to repair the item to the condition it was before the damage is repair cost. *D* refers to functional repair cost. *A* refers to the amount needed to replace the item. *C* is the description of actual cash value replacement.

9. C: A producer that has an agency relationship with an insurer can bind coverage, collect premiums, and assist with the claim process on behalf of the insurance company. Producers cannot determine what claim amounts should be.

10. B: The pair or set condition allows for payment to be made based on the value lost to the overall set if an individual piece is damaged.

11. B: A foreign company is a company doing business in a state other than its domicile state.

12. A: Earned premium is how much premium an insurer is due in a given period.

13. A: The endorsements section of a policy is where changes to a policy are listed.

14. D: Due to the vacancy clause, coverage for water, vandalism, theft, and glass would cease when the building has been vacant for 60 consecutive days or more.

Property Policy Provisions and Contract Law

Exclusions

Exclusions are the portion of an insurance policy that explain exactly what is *not* covered. These exclusions are listed because they are predictable, preventable, or are simply more than a company can afford to insure. Common exclusions include:

- **Non-accidental losses:** Insurance is used to protect against unforeseeable risks or accidents. Non-accidental losses are usually the result of predictable outcomes like normal wear and tear. Therefore, it is not a matter of if a loss will occur, but a matter of when. This is an uninsurable risk and excluded from insurance policies. For example, a computer monitor will eventually wear out from use, and the insured will have to purchase a new one. Though this may be considered a loss by the insured, it is a non-accidental loss because it happened from normal use, and, therefore, not covered by the property insurance policy.

- **Catastrophic losses:** Insurance companies usually diversify their exposure to loss. One way to do this is by insuring similar risks in different geographical regions so that most of the insured risks will not be exposed to the same event. A **catastrophic loss** is an event that exposes the company to more risk than they can cover. Events such as a war that exposes an entire country to catastrophic or huge losses are excluded from coverage.

- **Property already covered by other insurance:** This exclusion prohibits a property owner from insuring their property more than once, thus creating a moral hazard. There cannot be economic gain for the insured, only the protection of loss. For example, an insured cannot purchase insurance on their house from two insurance companies and then collect double the amount of any claims that are incurred. Doing so would be fraudulent.

- **Losses controllable by the insured:** These are exclusions that a policy owner could reasonably avoid. For instance, if an insured knows a step leading to their front door is broken and they do nothing to fix it, the insurance company may not pay the claim if a visitor is injured in a fall caused by the broken step. The insured, using common sense, should have known the broken step could cause injury and had it repaired.

- **Extra hazardous perils:** Events such as earthquakes and volcanic eruptions are extreme causes of loss. The likelihood of loss is usually too small to insure against, unless the property is in an area known to produce these types of losses. Coverage for these types of events can be acquired, but it usually involves additional premiums and special endorsements. For example, if an insured resides in an area that has no history of damage being caused by earthquakes, the insured may be able to purchase coverage for losses associated with an earthquake but would pay an additional premium for the coverage.

- **Liability perils:** This is when an insured is responsible for damage to another party, not themselves. There are some common exclusions to policies covering liability exposure.
    - Bodily Injury sustained by the insured. For example, if the store owner slips and falls in his own store, they cannot blame themselves for not putting up a sign.
    - Property damage created by the owner. For example, a property owner cannot purposely damage his own property and expect to hold himself liable.
    - Property damage when insured has custody of property. For example, a grocery store owner cannot expect his liability policy to pay for goods that he damaged after receiving them from a vendor.
    - Intentional injury inflicted by the insured. For example, if a property owner hits a guest over the head with a frying pan on purpose, he cannot expect his insurance company to pay for the injury.
    - Losses that are already covered by law, such as workers' compensation and Nuclear Energy Liability are also excluded from liability policies.

Conditions

All insurance policies have **conditions**, which explain the rights and obligations or duties each party has within the contract. In the conditions section of an insurance contract, the rights and duties of the insured and insurer are specifically stated. The conditions portion of a liability policy are listed the same as they are in a property policy. Some common conditions are as follows:

- **Duty after a loss** explains what an insured is responsible for should a claim arise. Some common conditions are notification of loss and timely delivery of information pertaining to the claim to the insurance company. Insureds are contractually obligated to provide the insurer with the information they need to examine the claim and decide what to pay, if anything. For example, if someone is injured while on your property, that could result in a potential claim, and you must notify your insurance company within a certain length of time.
- **Other insurance** describes how claims will be paid if there are multiple policies insuring the same liability. Traditionally, liability policies use an equal share contribution, which means the insurers will participate equally up to the limits of their respective policies.
- **Named insured** is what the person or entity to whom the policy is issued is called. The named insured does not have to be the only covered person or entity on a policy. There can be a first named insured, which is the person or entity who could experience a covered loss. There could also be additional insureds, which are other people or entities covered by the policy. Regardless of how many insureds are named on a policy, there will be a **policy limit**, which is the maximum amount the insurance company will pay. The policy limit is also referred to as a **limit of insurance, limit of coverage,** or **limit of liability.**

- An insured's **duties following a loss** include (but are not limited to):
    - Informing the insurance agent and/or insurance company of a loss claim event in a timely manner, also known as filing the claim. Insurance policies may be specific as to how much time an insured has to advise the company of a claim.
    - Making the property available for viewing, so representatives of the company, such as adjusters, can determine the value of the loss.
    - Aiding the company's representative(s) during inspection of the property, such as showing them where the loss occurred or providing requested documentation.
    - Providing a proof of loss statement, which documents all of the details pertaining to the loss.
    - Implementing measures to protect the property from further loss, such as covering a broken window or replacing a broken lock.
    - Submitting to examination under oath.

In addition, the insurance company has obligations to their policy holders. These obligations primarily deal with **valuation.** Valuation advises the insured what amount is to be paid following a claim and demonstrates how the insurance company determined the amount. Contributing factors to how losses will be paid include policy limits, insurable interest, actual cash value, replacement cost, and repair cost. Unless otherwise stated in the contract, the insurance company will usually retain the right to pay claims based on the lowest valuation.

Causes of Loss Forms

The **causes of loss forms** deal primarily with commercial property insurance and are categorized as basic, broad, and special.

The **cause of loss (basic form)** is divided into which perils are covered and which perils are excluded. Covered perils include lightning, fire (and extended coverages such as water damage incurred when the fire was being extinguished), explosion, windstorm or hail, aircraft, vehicles (except when owned or operated by the insured), riot, vandalism, sinkhole, volcanic eruption, sprinkler leakage, and smoke.

Excluded perils include laws and ordinances (unless covered by an endorsement), government action; fungus; bacteria; wet and dry rot (unless they result from fire or lightning); nuclear dangers; earth movement; war/military activity; acts of terrorism regardless of whether war is declared or not; power or utility service failure originating beyond the insured premises; mechanical breakdown; steam boiler, pipe, engine, or turbine explosion; artificial electrical current; water-related hazards; pipe rupture, except for automatic sprinklers; and water or steam leakage caused by the breakage of water or steam systems.

An insured may also have limited coverage for fungus, wet and dry rot, and bacteria as an additional coverage cause of loss (basic form). It covers damage resulting from fungus (which includes mold, mildew, spores, scents, mycotoxins, and fungal residue) and provides reimbursement for the following costs: removing mold and repairing direct physical property damage or loss caused by the mold, removing and replacing portions of the building so one can gain access to the mold, and testing to determine the presence of mold after property repairs or replacements have been completed. There is a limit to the reimbursement amount, and coverage only applies if the damage occurs during the policy period and the mold is caused by a covered loss.

It is the duty of the insured to prevent further damage where reasonably possible.

When considering covered and excluded perils, the covered perils are usually unpredictable events that cannot be prepared for, and other than riot and vandalism, do not have the prospect of human cause. Excluded perils often involve human cause, and in some instances, steps to avoid the loss can be taken.

The **cause of loss (broad form)** includes the covered and excluded perils of the cause of loss basic form with additional coverages for:

- Weight of ice, sleet or snow
- Falling objects (exterior damage only, unless the object pierces an outside wall and causes interior damage)
- Water damage from a damaged water system and the cost of removal and replacement of the damaged water system

The broad form also includes additional limited mold coverage and additional collapse coverage. Collapse must be the result of glass breakage, weight of people and/or personal property, weight of rain on the roof, hidden decay, and hidden insect/vermin damage that was unknown to the insured. It also covers collapse during construction if the building materials used are defective, and the collapse occurs during construction.

The additional collapse coverage on the cause of loss (broad form) also covers outdoor properties when they sustain direct damage from a collapsed building. The following structures are covered under collapse additional coverage:

- Radio/television antennas, satellite dishes, and their equipment
- Yard fixtures
- Awnings, gutters, and downspouts
- Piers, wharves, docks, etc.
- Fences
- Retaining walls
- Outdoor swimming pools
- Diving platforms
- Walks/roadways/paved surfaces

Even in the absence of building collapse, personal property collapse is covered, provided the property is inside the building, the collapse was caused by a named cause of loss, and the property is not one of the outdoor items listed above.

To receive coverage, the following items must be damaged by glass breakage or a cause of loss listed in the broad form:

- Valuable papers, records, storage media, drawings, and similar items
- Statuary, marble, porcelain, chinaware, and other fragile items
- Building machinery or equipment owned by the insured or in their care
- Animals that are killed

The **cause of loss (special form)** provides open peril protection against any direct physical loss not otherwise excluded under the policy. The following perils are excluded under the policy:

- Wear and tear, smog, fungus, rust, corrosion, deterioration, and any innate defects
- Mechanical breakdown
- Pollutant discharge (except when it is caused by a specific cause of loss)
- Insect, bird, or rodent damage
- Poor planning, development, design, workmanship, etc.
- Collapse not listed under collapse additional coverage
- Steam explosion (boilers, pipes, and engines)
- Settling, shrinking, expanding, and cracking
- Criminal or dishonest activities carried out by the insured or their employees/volunteers (regardless of whether or not those persons are being compensated by the insured)
- Damage caused by decisions and actions (including those acting on behalf of the insured)
- Damage caused by failing to make correct decisions or act appropriately (including those acting on behalf of the insured)
- Damage to personal property located outside the building caused by rain, ice, or snow
- Fraudulent or deceitful acts that cause the insured to lose property

The cause of loss (special form) also includes the limited mold additional coverage and the collapse additional coverage.

The cause of loss (special form) has the following coverage limitations:

- $2,500 limit on theft coverage for furs and garments lined with or made of fur
- $2,500 limit on theft coverage for dies, patterns, molds, and forms
- $2,500 limit on theft coverage for jewelry and watches worth more than $100, precious and semiprecious stones, jewels, gold, silver, and platinum
- $250 limit on theft coverage for stamps, credit letters, tickets, and lottery tickets for sale

As all insurance policy wordings vary, it is always imperative that the insurance agent be very familiar with the perils that are covered and those that are not.

When addressing the different cause of loss forms on the exam, it can be helpful to identify if the damage was caused by human error. Was the event that caused the damage predictable? Could reasonable steps have been taken to avoid the damage? If the answer to either of these questions is yes, then the loss is likely to be excluded. (This tip is provided as simply a guide and demonstrates the importance of common sense when it comes to what is and what is not covered in insurance policies.)

Conditions Pertaining to Personal Property Policies

As with commercial insurance policies, personal property policies (commonly referred to as homeowner's policies) have conditions. These conditions explain the rights and duties of both the insurance company and the insured.

The following are some of the key conditions of personal property policies.

Change conditions explain what changes can be allowed to a contract and what steps must be taken by either party to cause the change to occur. For example, if an insured makes improvements to a property that result in the property being worth substantially more money, and thus increasing the value it should be insured for, in the change conditions section it will state how long the insured has to notify the insurance company of the improvements.

Liberalization is a topic already covered. It allows the insurance company to broaden coverage to all policies of a similar class, without endorsement. Premiums cannot increase as a result of the additional coverage until the policy is renewed.

Concealment fraud is the condition that states the insured will not conceal or lie about the property to be insured. It also states that such actions can and most likely will null and void the insurance contract. When an insurance policy is considered null and void, it is the same as if the insurance policy never existed at all. For example, if the insured states their house is a single-family dwelling where they reside, and the dwelling is actually a rooming house rented to several people, and the insured lives somewhere else, this is concealment fraud and could result in the insurance policy being considered null and void.

Subrogation is the condition that gives an insurance company the right to pursue legal action against a party found to be at fault for damages they have paid for. Suppose a person breaks into a house and causes damage and is subsequently charged criminally and convicted for the crime. The insurance company may sue that person to recoup the money they paid to repair the damage they caused.

Policy period is the length or term of the insurance protection. Most personal property policies are issued for a term of one year.

Cancellation describes the conditions under which and insurance policy can be cancelled. An insurer has to give notice to the insured of the cancellation date as well as an explanation as to why a policy is being cancelled. A policy can be cancelled for any reason by the insurance company, provided the policy has been in force for 60 days or less, and the insurer provides ten days' written notice to the insured. If the insured materially misrepresents information, the insurer can cancel the policy provided thirty days' written notice is given to the insured. If the risk level of the policy changes, the insurer can cancel the policy, provided thirty days' written notice is given to the insured.

If the insured does not pay the agreed premium, the insurer can cancel the policy, provided ten days' written notice is given to the insured. Either party can elect not to renew the policy at the end of the policy term, which effectively cancels the policy on the renewal or anniversary date.

Sections of an Insurance Contract/Policy

- **Declaration** is the section that lists, or declares, information such as who owns the policy, the address of record, the cost of the policy (premium), description of what is insured, the amount of insurance, and the policy period.
- The **insuring agreement** further specifies the property covered, type of coverage, covered and excluded perils, and the amount of coverage.
- **Exclusions** list the perils (losses) that are not covered
- **Definitions** clarify the terms within the contract.

Characteristics of an Insurance Contract

An insurance contract obligates, or sticks, the insurance company to the cost of damage. As such, the insurance company has the power to write a contract that protects them from adverse risk and unnecessary loss. This is referred to as **adhesion**, which means to stick to something, and in this case, the contract sticks to the insurance company. The language is usually in favor of the company; the only power the insured has is the power of purchase. An insured does not have to purchase insurance from a company.

Insurance contracts are also **conditional contracts**, which means there are conditions that must be met in order for the contract to force the insurer into paying a claim. The conditions must be listed and agreed to by both parties. When an insured signs the insurance policy, pays a premium for the policy, or both, this constitutes that the insured accepts the contract as it is written. It is important that insurance agents require the insured to read the policy, including all of the conditions, so as to avoid misunderstandings by the insured.

A **personal** contract means that the agreement is covering a person and their personal property. It also means that payment can only be remitted to the named insureds or to someone who has an insured interest in the property, such as the mortgagee of the property.

All insurance contracts are **unilateral** because they are one sided in terms of payment. The insured can decide to quit paying premiums at any time with the only repercussion being that the policy is no longer in force. If the premiums are paid as agreed in the contract, the insurer must pay covered claims and cannot elect to cancel the policy without cause other than during the initial 60-day period (with 10 days' written notice). The insurer is the only party bound to perform in the contract, making it unilateral in nature.

The contract also relies on **utmost good faith,** which means that both parties have and will deal with each other fairly and honestly. In short, the insurer agrees to pay claims for insured perils, and the insured agrees to make honest claims and statements.

Rating an Insurance Policy

Premium rates for insurance policies are based on three categories:

- **Judgment rating** is one of the earliest methods used when calculating premiums. This method relies on the underwriters' assessment of the risk based on the company's experience.
- **Manual rating,** or **class rating**, is a second method of categorizing risk. An underwriter will place the risk in accordance with the risk tables listed in their underwriting guide. The premium is based on a per-thousand basis in accordance with the table. For example, the cost to insure brick veneer homes of a certain age would be listed as $5 for every $1,000 of coverage. An underwriter will multiply the number of thousands of dollars of coverage by five, to calculate the premium for the insurance provided.
- **Merit rating** is a method where an underwriter uses credits for positive factors and debits for negative factors in order to determine the risk rating.

Underwriters usually use a combination of all rating methods when calculating insurance policy premiums.

Cancelling an Insurance Policy

An insured can easily cancel a policy by providing written notice to the insurer or by simply not paying the premium. If an insured has paid some or all of the policy premiums, it is beneficial for the insured to notify the insurer that they are cancelling their insurance policy as of a certain date, as the insured may get a refund for any unearned premiums.

Insurance companies have two tables that allow them to calculate the amount they will refund an insured in the event that an insurance policy is cancelled. **Short-rate** and **pro-rata** tables give the percentage of the unearned premium that is due to the insured in the event of a cancellation. Short-rate rebates return less of a percentage to the insured than pro-rata rebates.

Unearned premiums are usually refunded to the insured on a short-rate basis, meaning the company keeps a portion of the unearned premiums to offset their expenses. If an insured cancels their policy due to certain conditions, such as if they are moving out of state, the insurance company may refund the insured on a pro-rata basis.

An insurer does not have the right to cancel the policy unless there are violations of the conditions named in the policy. Even in the presence of violations of conditions that warrant policy cancellation, the company must provide the insured written notification and may be required to repay the unused premiums on a pro-rata basis.

A company can use a **flat cancellation,** which cancels on its effective date. This is typically done within the first 60 days of the contract and still requires written notification. The insurance company can elect not to renew the policy on the expiry or anniversary date, which is known as a **non-renewal.**

Fair Credit Reporting Act

Credit reports are sometimes used as part of the underwriting process.

The reports are classified as **consumer** or **investigative,** the only difference being that investigative reports involve interviews with the consumer's associates. The reports cannot include bankruptcy information beyond 10 years, or legal actions beyond 7 years.

If an insurance company wishes to order an investigative consumer report, they must provide written notice to the applicant within 3 days of the order. The fair credit reporting act also provides for the applicant to dispute information contained in the report, and if the information caused an increase in premiums, the insurer must provide a written explanation as to what information caused the increase.

Credit reports have become an important part of the underwriting process. If an insured is having difficulty meeting their financial obligations, this may increase the possibility that the insured could submit a fraudulent claim in order to gain access to funds.

Practice Questions

1. The loss ratio is determined by:
    a. Incurred losses divided by the total earned premium
    b. Expenses divided by the total premium collected
    c. The total policies cancelled pro rata
    d. Combining the total of all collected premiums

2. Who is responsible for protecting a damaged property from incurring further damage after a loss?
    a. The agent
    b. The insured
    c. The adjuster
    d. The insurance company

3. Which of the following is NOT a cause of loss form?
    a. Broad Form
    b. Basic Form
    c. Special Form
    d. Open Form

4. In which section of an insurance contract would you find the address of record for the owner of the policy?
    a. Declarations
    b. Insuring Agreement
    c. Exclusions
    d. Definitions

5. When can a company cancel a policy?
    a. Anytime, but it must provide 60 days' written notice
    b. Within the first 60 days for any reason, but it must provide written notice
    c. When the earned premium has been satisfied
    d. Only after the pro-rata rebate

6. Which method of rating uses a credit/debit method of determining rates?
    a. Class rating
    b. Judgment rating
    c. Merit rating
    d. Manual rating

7. What condition allows a company to pursue legal action against a third party found to be at fault?
    a. Liberalization condition
    b. Concealment fraud condition
    c. Subrogation condition
    d. Estoppel condition

8. The pro-rata condition of a policy is applicable when:
   a. The insured owns a policy insuring multiple properties
   b. The insured has two policies insuring the same property
   c. The claim is larger than the aggregate coverage
   d. There are multiple named insureds

9. What portion of a policy lists the perils not covered?
   a. Declarations
   b. Valuations
   c. Exclusions
   d. Standards

10. Which of the following components is NOT necessary to be a legal and binding agreement?
   a. Competent parties
   b. Offer and acceptance
   c. Legal purpose
   d. Notarized signatures

11. Insurance contracts are _______ in nature, which means one party has more power to establish terms and conditions than the other.
   a. Unilateral
   b. Fiduciary
   c. Bilateral
   d. Multilingual

12. If an agent offers a portion of his commission to an unlicensed client as an inducement to buy a policy from them, the agent has committed __________.
   a. Counter-signment
   b. Rebating
   c. Twisting
   d. Fraud

13. When an insured misrepresents facts pertaining to the property insured and a claim is paid as a result of the misrepresented facts, the insured has committed:
   a. Material misrepresentation
   b. Fraud
   c. Concealment
   d. Breach of contract

14. Which of the following acts is prohibited by an agent who does not have an agency relationship with a carrier?
   a. Bind coverage
   b. Explain the policy terms and conditions
   c. Accept premiums
   d. Assist with claims

15. The policy period is best described by which answer?
    a. How long the coverage will be in force
    b. How long subrogation will take
    c. How long a peril is covered
    d. How long the property has been mortgaged

16. An insurance policy is considered to be a:
    a. Contract
    b. Claim form
    c. Federal regulation
    d. Aggregate

17. Who does an agent of an insurer represent?
    a. The customer
    b. The insurance company
    c. The commissioner
    d. The adjuster

Answer Explanations

1. A: The loss ratio is found by dividing the incurred loss by the earned premium. The expense ratio is found by dividing expenses by total premium. Answers C and D are not valid formulas for performance.

2. B: Under the duties of insured condition of an insurance contract, it is the duty of the insured to protect their property from further damage. Neither the agent, the insurance company, nor the adjuster is responsible for protecting the property from further damage.

3. D: Broad, basic, and special are the loss forms used to file claims. Open form is not an applicable answer.

4. A: The declarations section of the contract includes information such as the name of the owner, address of record, property insured, and premium charged. The insuring agreement describes details about the covered and excluded perils. The exclusions section lists loss events that are not covered. The definitions section defines the terms within the contract.

5. B: An insurer can cancel a policy within the first 60 days of the policy if it provides written notification to the insured.

6. C: Merit rating is when an underwriter takes into account the positive and negative factors associated with the risk to be insured.

7. C: The subrogation condition allows an insurer to pursue legal action against a third party found to be at fault.

8. B: When there are two policies insuring the same property, companies can participate in claims in proportion to the amount of coverage they respectively provide.

9. C: The exclusions section of a policy lists the perils that are excluded from coverage.

10. D: A contract must have competent parties, an offer and acceptance, a legal purpose, and consideration (payment), to be legal and binding. Notarized signatures can be required by a party but are not necessary to meet the criteria of a legal contract such as an insurance policy.

11. A: Insurance contracts are unilateral in nature because the insurance company sets the terms under which they will pay a claim.

12. B: If an agent offers a portion of their commission to an unlicensed client, that is rebating.

13. B: While misrepresenting facts knowingly or unknowingly is material misrepresentation, when a claim is paid as a result of the act, it becomes fraud.

14. A: An agent who is appointed with a carrier, but not under an agency relationship, can perform any of the listed acts except bind coverage.

15. A: The policy period details how long the coverage will be in force.

16. A: All insurance policies are contracts.

17. B: The agent is a representative of the insurance company.

Types of Casualty Policies and Bonds

Types of Casualty Insurance

Casualty insurance applies to personal and commercial policies and covers losses sustained by third parties. Casualty insurance can be included as part of a policy that covers other types of losses or be issued on a stand-alone basis. Types of casualty insurance coverages include the following:

- Automotive insurance—personal and commercial
- Commercial general liability
- Workers' compensation
- Commercial crime liability
- Employment practices liability
- Personal and commercial umbrella liability
- Public liability
- Product liability
- Professional liability

Automotive Insurance

Automotive insurance pays for claims that result from personal or commercial vehicles that cause bodily injury or property damage to a third party.

Personal Auto Insurance

Personal auto insurance policies provide coverage for private passenger automobiles, meaning vehicles not used for business purposes. Auto policies contain different coverage categories:

- **Part A:** Covers liability for bodily injury and property damage to third parties. This coverage is mandatory in many states.
- **Part B**: Coverage for medical payments (optional in many states)
- **Part C:** Mandatory coverage for uninsured motorist
- **Part D:** Optional coverage for physical damage (known as collision and comprehensive) to the insured's auto. This coverage can be mandatory if there is a lien or money owed on the vehicle. An important distinction about the mandatory coverage is that it can be required by the lien holder, but it is not a mandatory coverage required by the insurer.
- **Part E**: Duties after a loss
- **Part F**: General provisions

If the insured purchases a vehicle that will replace an insured vehicle on the policy, known as a substitution, the new vehicle will have the same coverages as the deleted vehicle. If the insured purchases an additional vehicle, it will be automatically covered for the same coverages that are on the primary vehicle on the policy. For either of these 2 coverages to remain valid, the insured must notify the insurer of the changes within 30 days. When an insured vehicle is driven outside your state of residence and within North America, if the insured is at fault for a claim under liability, coverage will be increased, if necessary, to meet the minimum required liability limit, by law, for that state or province.

Other coverages like towing/roadside assistance and car rental may be added by endorsements and are subject to additional premiums.

Commercial Automobile Insurance/Business Auto Coverage Insurance

Commercial automobile insurance, also referred to as **business auto coverage insurance,** is purchased by businesses to cover the vehicles they use to conduct their operations. Commercial automobile insurance coverage is required if a business owns, leases, or rents vehicles or if vehicles they do not own are used during their course of business. Specific coverage forms are available to insure vehicles in varying categories for certain additional coverages. Liability coverage is provided for the insured and employees, partners, members, and others while they are driving vehicles owned by the business or their own vehicles while conducting duties directly related to the business. Coverage for physical damage, medical payments, uninsured and underinsured motorist, if not included, are available for an additional premium.

Commercial or business automobiles are identified by numbers when listed on an insurance policy. These numbers are applicable only to insurance policies. Covered **automobile identification numbers** are defined as:

1. Any automobile used for business purposes
2. Automobiles owned by the business
3. Private passenger automobiles owned by the business
4. Automobiles classed other than private passenger
5. Automobiles that must carry "no fault" insurance in the state where they are insured
6. Automobiles that must carry uninsured motorist coverage in the state where they are insured
7. Individually described automobiles, possibly subject to additional premiums
8. Automobiles that are leased, rented, borrowed, or hired that are used by but not owned by the business. Excluded from this identification number are automobiles owned by employees, members (if the business is a limited liability company), partners (if the business is a partnership), or vehicles owned by members of their households
9. Non-owned private passenger classed vehicles that are owned by any person acting on behalf of a company and used by that person to conduct business for the company. Since personal automobile policies exclude business use, third party liability, bodily injury, and property damage incurred while the person is operating their personal automobile for company purposes, these non-owned vehicles are provided for under commercial auto insurance policies.
10. Vehicles classed as mobile equipment that must be insured by law

Commercial automobile policies provide liability coverage for **trailers** that are not owned by the business but are being towed by a vehicle that is covered under the policy. Losses are restricted to trailers with a load capacity of 2000 pounds or less that are designed for use on public roads, and the trailer must be attached to the insured auto at the time the damage occurs. For example, a half ton truck owned and insured by the business is towing a utility trailer. While making a turn, the trailer slides and damages a light pole. Coverage to repair the light pole would be afforded under the company's commercial automobile insurance policy.

If a business has multiple vehicles, they may purchase a **fleet policy** which allows for several vehicles, sometimes with different classifications, to be insured under one policy. For example, a construction company or a bus company may use a fleet policy.

All motor carriers, or trucking companies, in the United States are required, by law, to have liability coverage for bodily injury and property damage to third parties. The **Motor Carrier Act** (MCA) of 1980 enacted a statute that if motor carriers could not prove they had enough funds in reserve to be considered self-insured, they would have to have the MCS90 endorsement filed with the government in order to operate. This endorsement provides liability coverage, including environmental restitution, with a minimum limit ranging from $750,000 to $5,000,000 depending on the commodities being transported. Additional motor carriage insurance to cover physical damage, medical payments, uninsured motorist, and cargo is available for purchase.

Commercial Automobile Insurance Policy Exclusions

In addition to the exclusions pertaining to all insurance policies, losses occurring as a consequence of the following, when any person is operating a vehicle for business purposes, is excluded:

- Contractual liability (except when the loss would have not happened if a contract were present)
- Damage to or caused by property that is being transported (optional transit insurance is available for purchase)
- Damage that occurs while property is being loaded or unloaded (optional coverage sold separately)
- Damage as the result of the operation of mobile equipment (coverage is available under a commercial general liability policy)
- Caused by any pollution
- Arising as a result of completed operations
- As a result of employee indemnification and employer's liability (coverage is available under a separate insurance policy)
- Due to the movement of any property by a mechanical device (other than a hand truck)

Commercial auto liability insurance policies often contain more than one type of coverage form. There are four types of commercial auto policies:

- **Business auto**: Provides liability coverage for any vehicle that is owned, leased, borrowed, or hired by the business
- **Garage coverage**: Protects auto-related businesses that repair, service, sell, store, or park vehicles

- **Truckers coverage**: Protects common carriers
- **Business auto physical damage**: Covers physical damage to business-owned autos for collision, comprehensive claims—e.g., fire, theft, glass, hail—and towing

Commercial General Liability

Commercial general liability (CGL) protects businesses from bodily injury and property damage claims that are associated with business. All businesses have inherent liability exposures that make them vulnerable to lawsuits by third parties. Liability claims may result from business operations, products, completed operations, and advertising and personal injury liability.

Commercial general liability policies provide liability coverage under the categories of property damage and bodily injury, medical payments, personal and advertising injury liability, and tenants legal liability. As with any insurance policy, there are perils excluded from coverage under a commercial general liability policy. Additional liability insurance policies covering the excluded perils may be available for purchase. For example, Directors and Officers (D&O), Errors and Omissions (E&O), Environmental Impairment, and Employment Practices.

Commercial general liability policies may be issued under an occurrence form or a claims-made form. There are four types of commercial general liability insurance forms.

- **Premises and Operations:** This covers losses that occur on the physical premises or as a result of operations of an insured. Losses must occur within the territory stated in the declarations section.
- **Products Liability:** This covers losses that result from goods or merchandise that the business manufactures, sells, handles, distributes, or disposes. This covers the insured, individuals under the direction of the business, employees, and contractors of the business.
- **Completed Operations:** This covers losses connected to services to customers that are completed including product installation, construction, and repairs. This coverage begins when the work is completed, and the insured has left the worksite.
- **Contingent Liability:** This covers losses for the actions of others who are under the direction or control of the insured. This includes contractors or others having a contractual relationship with the business as outlined in a service contract, hold harmless agreement, lease agreement, or indemnification agreement.

Commercial General Liability Insurance Terms and Definitions

An automobile is a vehicle with four wheels and a gas or diesel internal combustion engine, designed for operation on roadways designated for normal vehicle use with their primary purpose being for transportation. **Automobiles** may still be classified as such even with the addition of certain components attached to the vehicle. For example, snow plows, air compressors, welding equipment, spraying equipment, and cherry pickers. As long as the attached implements cannot move on a road on their own, they do not alter the vehicle from being classed as an automobile.

Specifically, in regard to a commercial insurance policy, when a vehicle is used primarily for tasks such as lifting large items, digging, and scraping, it is considered to be **mobile equipment.** Even though the vehicle is transported over roadways designated for normal vehicle use, since transportation is not the primary purpose of the vehicle, it is classed as being mobile equipment. Types of mobile equipment include, but are not limited to:

- Fork lifts
- Tractors
- Farm machinery
- Front end loaders/diggers
- Back hoe
- Dump truck
- Road grader
- Steam roller
- Lighting equipment

With this specific classification, an automobile cannot also be titled as mobile equipment. For the purposes of commercial insurance policies, automobiles and mobile equipment are exclusive of one another. When registering a vehicle with a state's motor vehicle department, they are not described as being either an automobile or mobile equipment. Motor vehicle departments register any motorized conveyance that can be driven on a roadway as a vehicle. Separate automobile and motorized equipment classifications are strictly insurance terms when it comes to defining vehicle use.

An insured's products consist of items or services provided by the insured. Included are products and services that are the insured's property but are in the control of a person acting under the guise of the insured's business. If a product is manufactured, sold, distributed, handled, or disposed of they are deemed to be the insured's products. Excluding real property, which is defined as property that is attached to the land such as a buildings and permanent free-standing signs, insured's products incorporate the following:

- All components that are part of the products, even if they can be removed and reattached.
- Instructions, warnings, and other documents that are intended to be included with the product, even if those items did not accompany the product.
- Representations and warranties directly related to the product.

Whether it is carried out by the insured or their designate acting on behalf of their business, work related activities are deemed to be the insured's work. Included in the insured's work are the following:

- Additional information intended to be included with the insured's work. The information can consist of things like instructions and warnings.
- Components used in performing the insured's work products such as parts, materials, and equipment.
- Documents which guarantee the quality of the insured's work including research, representation, and warranties.

When an insured provides a product or service to property owned by a customer and the customer's product cannot be used for the intended purpose, it becomes **impaired property.** Commercial general liability policies will not cover the loss of use of the customer's product due to the fact that the property can be repaired. For example, ABC Manufacturing Company manufacturers computer processing chips. 123 Computer Company buys ABC Manufacturing's computer chips, installs them into their own computers, and sells the computers. Two weeks later, all of the computers have been returned to 123 Computer Company due to a defect with the computer chips provided by ABC Manufacturing Company. 123 Computer Company has suffered a loss; however, the claim will not be covered under ABC Manufacturing Company's commercial general liability insurance policy. Though they are defective, the computer chips can be replaced thus allowing 123 Computer Company to sell the computers again. 123 Computer Company did incur an economic loss, but insurance is intended to cover tort liability as opposed to contractual liability. There have been an abundance of legal action concerning impaired property, and it remains one of the most litigated coverages.

When a loss occurs somewhere other than on the insured's business premises and after the insured has completed a contractual obligation, coverage is excluded under the **products-completed operations hazard** portion of the commercial general insurance policy. For example, the insured is a roofing contractor hired to replace the roof on a customer's home. While the job is being done, coverage will exist for insured perils as long as the insured has purchased the coverage available under a variety of commercial insurance policies. If, six months after the roof has been completed, the customer is walking on their roof and falls through, causing bodily injury to themselves, under the products-completed operations hazard clause, there would be no coverage for their injuries even if the roofing contractor was negligent for their injuries. Optional commercial insurance policies to cover third party losses can be purchased to provide coverage for certain perils that occur after the completion of work by the insured. Usually limited to a certain time frame, often 24 months, available commercial liability insurance policies that will cover some perils are wrap-up liability and completed-operations.

When an insured pays a staffing firm to provide him with employees, and the staffing firm handles the employee's wages, taxes, and benefits, those employees are considered to be **leased workers.**

When a permanent employee is off work due to illness, holidays, or other reasons, employers hire **temporary workers** to perform the regular employee's duties. Temporary workers are paid wages by the employer, but they do not have the promise of an agreement or contract that guarantees them a certain amount of work. In addition, if an employer hires workers only for a specified period of time to perform seasonal work or assist with a one-time or special project, they are also known as temporary workers.

Persons who work for the insured without earning wages or compensation are regarded as **volunteer workers.** While wages are traditionally how workers are paid, employers need to be cautious about providing volunteer workers with free products or bartering with them for services as any form of payment has value and could be construed as payment for services or work rendered during litigation.

People who are working for the insured on a regular and permanent basis are defined as **employees.** For the purposes of insurance, leased workers are also considered to be employees, however, temporary and volunteer workers are not.

Pollutants are products which materialize in a solid, liquid, gaseous, or thermal form that are characterized as irritants or contaminants. **Pollutants** include, but are not limited to, chemicals, alkalis, smoke, soot, fumes, vapors, and waste. Substances that are waiting to be recycled, reconditioned, or reclaimed are identified as **waste**.

Property is **loading or uploading** under the following circumstances:

- Property is waiting to be moved onto a land vehicle, watercraft, or aircraft
- Property that is in the process of being loaded onto a vehicle, watercraft, or aircraft
- Property that is being moved around while it is on a vehicle, watercraft, or aircraft
- Property that is in the process of being unloaded from a vehicle, watercraft, or aircraft

When a business rents or leases their premises, **tenants legal liability** provides coverage for insured perils such as fire, smoke, and water damage. Only the damage to the property that is rented or leased is covered under tenants legal liability.

Commercial General Liability Policy Sections

Coverage A - Bodily Injury and Property Damage Liability

Losses that cause bodily injury and/or property damage to a third party occurring as a consequence of the insured(s) operating a business are covered, provided they arise from an insured peril and the insured is negligent, or at fault for, the claim. Policies are issued on an occurrence or claims-made basis. Losses must be accidental, defined as being unintentional. For example, an employee stacks tomatoes in a bin at a grocery store. A customer trips on a tomato that has fallen on the floor and breaks their ankle. Accidents can also include repeated exposure to common detrimental elements. For example, a contractor installs a window in a customer's building but fails to adequately seal it. Over the course of two weeks, rain leaks, unnoticed, into the room four times causing damage to the property. If the insured is covered for this peril, it would be regarded as a single loss, not four separate losses.

Coverage A - Bodily Injury and Property Damage Liability - Exclusions

In addition to the exclusions that are common to all insurance policies, bodily injury and property damage liability resulting from the following are also excluded from coverage on a commercial general liability policy:

- If the insured is required to pay damages pursuant to a contract
- If the insured sells, distributes, or produces any product containing liquor, there is no coverage resulting in damages by the third party's use of the liquor
- Any claim by an individual considered to be employed by the insured or by a member of the employee's family. This exclusion includes claims by a third party that the employer must share the cost of damages incurred by an employee of the insured
- Losses caused by any autos, aircraft, or watercraft owned by the insured
- Claims resulting from mobile equipment IF it is being used in any kind of planned speed or stunt activity or occurring while it is being transported
- Property that is occupied, owned, or rented by the insured
- Damage to the insured's owned products
- Losses occurring after the insured has completed work
- Damaged to impaired property or as a result of recalls due to actual or suspected defects

- Personal and advertising injuries
- Electronic data, including corruption, deletion, failure to operate, inability to access or loss of use
- Products sold or distributed that are in violation of any statute

Coverage B - Personal and Advertising Liability

This section provides liability coverage arising from intentional torts, defined as actions that are deliberate in nature. Though it is true that most insurance coverage is for losses that are unintentional, there are incidences when purposeful actions will be covered. As it pertains to personal and advertising liability, this coverage is very specific in that claimants suffer losses associated with acts such as having their rights violated or their reputation harmed as opposed to injuries that are more physical in nature. An example of personal injury is if a landlord believes a tenant has a cache of weapons in their apartment and enters the tenant's apartment when they are not home and without their knowledge, the tenant may sue the insured believing their privacy has been violated. An example of advertising injury is if a manufacturer of ABC Widgets states in their advertising that they are better than 123 Widgets because 123 Widgets have harmed thousands of people. The manufacturer of 123 Widgets sues ABC Widgets saying their advertising negatively impacted their sales. If it is proven that the manufacturer of ABC Widgets, the insured, received incorrect information, then they could be held libel for 123 Widget's losses.

Coverage B - Personal and Advertising Liability - Exclusions

Personal and advertising liability coverage is excluded for the following:

- Intentionally and maliciously violating another's rights
- Publishing materials known to be false by the insured
- If the insured is required to pay damages pursuant to a contract
- Losses from the insured's advertising statements failing to perform
- When advertisements depict pricing errors
- Any materials published prior to the commencement of the current policy period
- Breach of contract
- When the insured's business is an Internet or media type. For example, website design, search engines, publishing, broadcasting
- Trademark, copyright, trade secret, or patent
- Postings or ads on boards or electronic chat rooms that are owned, hosted, or controlled by the insured

- Losses incurred as a result of the insured intentionally engaging in the use of a name or product owned by a third party

- Claims arising directly or indirectly from the insured engaging in any unfair competition, violation of privacy statues, misappropriation, or infringement

Coverage C - Medical Payments
When an accident occurs at the insured's place of business or work site, medical payments can be paid to claimants, regardless as to whom is at fault for the injury. This coverage is offered at the discretion of the insurer.

Coverage C - Medical Payment - Exclusions
Medical payments for bodily injury coverage is excluded from the following:

- Incurred by the insured
- Incurred by any person considered to be in the employment of the insured UNLESS they are classified as volunteers
- Persons normally occupying the premises
- Any loss as a direct result of engaging in athletic activities
- Losses already covered under the products-completed operations hazard
- Any exclusions under Coverage A

Workers' Compensation Insurance

By 1949, the National Council on Compensation Insurance (NCCI) had established workers' compensation insurance to pay for work-related injuries to employees. **Workers' compensation** does not pay for non-work-related injuries. When a workers' compensation claim is filed, the insurer presumes that the insured was negligent. Payments are made without regard to proof of negligence.

Certain classes of workers are exempt from workers' compensation claims—e.g., agricultural workers, domestic workers, officers and directors of corporations, sole proprietors, and self-employed workers.

States form their own, specific laws regarding workers' compensation, including whether it is required in that state. Most states require that immigrant workers be covered under workers' compensation policies.

The definition of a **workers' compensation injury** includes sickness, illness, disability or death caused by a work-related accident or occurrence. Workers are entitled to receive lost wages or income, medical payments, rehabilitation, and survivors' benefits.

If any of the following are applicable, the employer can be held responsible for any damages incurred by their employee:

- Intentional misconduct by the employer
- Any discrimination against any employee that is in violation of any law
- Employers failing to conform to workplace safety or health regulations
- When the employer knowingly violates any law

When an employee claims **workers' compensation benefits**, they generally forfeit their right to sue their employer for the injuries they incurred. Workers' compensation benefits are an integral part of the insurance industry amounting to approximately $63.6 billion in claims in the United States in 2013, costing employers an average of $1.37 per $100 of covered wages. The following table from the U.S. Department of Labor, Bureau of Labor Statistics presents the ten occupations with the largest number of injuries and illnesses for 2013*.

Rank	Occupation	Number	Percent of Total
1	Laborers (nonconstruction)	53,740	5.9%
2	Truck drivers, heavy and tractor trailer	49,000	5.3
3	Nursing assistants	41,450	4.5
4	Janitors and cleaners	39,040	4.3
5	General maintenance and repair workers	28,460	3.1
6	Police and sheriff's patrol officers	28,170	3.1
7	Registered nurses	27,020	2.9
8	Retail salespersons	26,830	2.9
9	Light truck and delivery service drivers	23,980	2.6
10	Stock clerks and order fillers	22,710	2.5
	Total, Top 10	340,400	37.1%
	Total, All Occupations	917,090	100%

*Nonfatal injuries and illnesses involving days off from work for private industries; excludes farms with fewer than 11 employees.

Commercial Crime Insurance

Commercial crime insurance, also known as **fidelity insurance**, is a broad term that refers to crimes committed against a business or organization, both on and off premises, that result in financial losses to the business. Crime insurance policies protect against theft, fraud, and dishonesty by employees or third parties.

Crime policies are purchased either on a discovery or loss sustained basis. **Discovery** policies state that losses must be discovered during the policy period, or within 60 days of expiration (unless a new policy is issued) but can be covered no matter when the loss occurred. For example, if it is discovered during an audit that an individual forged the insured's name in order to embezzle funds from the business six months ago, but the current policy has only been in force for two months, the loss could be covered under the current policy. **Loss sustained** policies state that losses must have occurred and been discovered during the current policy period, or within a year of the policy's expiration date. Loss sustained policies include a loss sustained during prior insurance condition which allows coverage for losses that occurred during the previous policy period, even if the loss is discovered during the current policy period, if the following three conditions are met:

- Both crime policies cover the loss as an insured peril
- The discovery period has ended for the previous policy
- The current policy period is consecutive to the prior policy period

Coverage for the following losses are insured under crime policies, though they may have provisions attached to the losses:

- Money and securities (including if lost, damaged, destroyed, or stolen while in the possession of a third party such as an armored car company or private messenger)
- Inside and outside robbery
- Money orders and counterfeit money
- Depositor's forgery
- Burglary that involves forcible entry (including safes)
- Computer fraud
- Fraud coverage for funds transfer
- Employee theft

Coverage for the following may be available for purchase under a separate insurance policy or an endorsement on the current crime policy:

- Losses from a safety deposit box
- Extortion (losses that include threats of bodily harm)
- Fraudulent impersonation (losses as a result of someone impersonating an employee, customer, or vendor)
- Virtual Currency (types of currency that have the same value as traditional money but exist in a virtual state that may not be government regulated, such as Bitcoin)

Coverage for the following losses are excluded. Coverage may be available under a separate policy or endorsement:

- Committed by the owner, partners (if the business is a partnership) or members (if the business is a limited liability company)
- Accounting errors and omissions
- Voluntary participation in property exchange or purchase (even is deception occurred)
- Fire (example - cash burns in a fire)
- Vending machine/money operated equipment (coin washer and dryer) unless it records the amount deposited
- Vandalism
- Embezzlement
- Damage to any motor vehicle
- Theft by any employee when the employer is aware of prior thefts by the employee
- Confidential information (for example, losses due to the disclosure of a customer's information)

- Inventory (pertaining to loss of income or clients due to inventory not being available, defective, etc.)
- Any government action
- Mergers and acquisitions
- Investments, trading, stocks
- Criminal fines and penalties

When losses occur outside of the listed **coverage territory**, coverage is usually available worldwide as long as the employee is not outside the coverage territory for more than 90 days.

Employment Practices Liability

Employment practices liability policies protect an employer against claims brought by potential, current, or former employees as a result of perceived practices by the employer. These types of claims include discrimination, wrongful termination or dismissal, failure to promote, invasion of privacy, deprivation of a career opportunity, negligent employee evaluation, and sexual harassment.

Coverage is provided for directors and officers, management, personnel, and all other employees. Exclusions of coverage usually include bodily injury, property damage, intentional acts, and dishonest acts.

Employment practices liability policies are issued on a claims-made basis. Supplementary payments are deducted from the aggregate limit of the policy, meaning all costs to defend a claim are subtracted from the liability limit of the policy.

Personal and Commercial Umbrella Liability

Personal and commercial umbrella liability policies are issued to provide liability coverage in the event of a large claim by increasing the amount of liability coverage. If a claim is settled for more than the limit of coverage on an insured's policy, an **umbrella liability** policy "drops down" to cover the additional amount up to the limit of the **umbrella policy**. For example, a third-party claim for injuries sustained in an auto accident for which the insured was at fault was settled for $1,500,000. The insured had a liability limit of $1,000,000 on his or her auto policy and a $5,000,000 limit on an umbrella liability policy; the umbrella liability policy would cover the extra $500,000.

Umbrella liability policies may also offer coverage that is excluded on the insured's other liability policy, such as malicious prosecution, false arrest, mental anguish, slander, and libel.

Public Liability

Public liability policies are generally purchased to cover damage to a third party when the insured is involved in an event that is held in a building he or she does not own and where members of the public will be in attendance. Purchase of a public liability policy may be required when someone rents a hall to hold an event, such as a wedding reception or business conference. For some personal and commercial policies, coverage for public liability may be provided in certain circumstances and may be available as an endorsement for a single event at an additional premium. An example where a public liability policy could provide coverage is if a guest slips on the dance floor and is injured at a wedding reception.

Product Liability

If a company sells, distributes, repairs, or manufactures products, they would purchase **product liability** insurance to protect them in the event a third party sustains property damage or injury while using their product. Product liability covers instances that occur as a result of product defects, missing or improper instructions, warnings, and toxic materials. Common exclusions on product liability policies include the following:

- Efficacy: A product that fails to do as promised, such as a cold and flu medication from a pharmaceutical company that fails to relieve sinus pressure
- Material: A product that is manufactured using a known toxin or prohibited ingredient
- Quality control: Failure on the part of the policy holder to properly oversee distribution of their product

Depending on the product being covered, exclusions will usually be tailored specifically for an individual policy. An example of a third-party claim under a product liability policy would be if the battery in a person's mobile device caught fire and caused damage to other property or bodily injury.

Professional Liability

Professional liability policies are purchased by those whose careers are regarded as professional in nature and, in some instances, may have a professional designation. Professionals who purchase this coverage include doctors, lawyers, accountants, and insurance agents. Some states require that certain professionals have professional liability coverage in order to practice.

Professional liability provides coverage for claims resulting from negligence, malpractice, and errors. Professional liability insurance is also known as **errors and omissions** and **malpractice** insurance. An example of damages that could be suffered from a third party and covered under a professional liability policy might be financial losses resulting from an error in calculations by an accountant who prepared an individual's tax return, a post-operative infection suffered by the patient of a surgeon, or an insurance agent who forgets to add an endorsement to a policy.

Specific Liability Policies

In addition to commercial general liability policies and liability coverage provided under personal automobile and personal property policies, specific liability policies and endorsements covering certain liability exposures are available. As with all insurance policies, these liability coverages will be subject to policy provisions, including insured perils, limitations of coverage, and exclusions. In addition to liability exposures detailed in this manual, popular liability policies include:

- **Advertising Liability**: Covers losses arising from the insured's advertising of their products and services. For example, copyright infringement, plagiarism slander, libel, privacy issues, and patent protection.
- **Builder's Risk**: Provided for professionals such as contractors, developers, and skilled trades, coverage is for damage that occurs at a location other than the insured's office, such as at a construction site or storage facility.

- **Business Owners Policy (BOP)**: Usually purchased by small businesses with special coverages for uncommon or unique exposures. For example, liability coverage for an office, visited by customers, located in the insured's rented premises in a strip mall or for an insured who is operating a business outside regular classifications. These policies are almost always accompanied by distinct endorsements adding and/or limiting specific coverage.

- **Cyber Liability**: Coverage for businesses who handle information electronically. Data breaches and other cyber crime activity has necessitated the recommendation that businesses obtain this type of liability insurance. These policies are constantly evolving due to the ongoing technological advancement.

- **Directors and Officers Liability (D&O)**: Coverage for claims against directors and officers of a company. For-profit and not-for-profit businesses both purchase this coverage for losses generally arising from negative implications realized as a result of the actions of the directors and officers. It is important to note that coverage for this type of liability exposure will cover insured perils arising directly from the director's and officer's duties as they relate to their role in the business. No protection is available for any actions that are related to any other activities. For example, a doctor is a member of a community services board and is sued for malpractice by a patient. Because they are being sued due to their actions as a doctor which have nothing to do with their duties as a member of the community services board, there would be no coverage for the doctor.

- **Environmental Liability**: Purchased by companies who use possible toxic substances in their business which includes storing, producing, processing, transporting, or otherwise being in control of products that may be harmful to the environment. Coverage includes losses related to these materials in regard to third party bodily injury and property damage, legal expenses, and, possibly, clean up costs.

- **Errors and Omissions Liability (E&O)**: Insures losses sustained as a result of unintentional negligent actions that lead to financial losses sustained by a third party. Errors and omissions insurance can be extended to cover bodily injury and property damage incurred by a third party. Errors and omissions liability is an essential coverage for businesses that engage in any form of client service as it covers perils such as unintentional warranty breaches, misrepresentations, and human errors. For example, a client requests an endorsement to cover the cost of a car rental in the event their vehicle is not drivable due to a claim. Their insurance agent forgets to add this coverage. Several months later, the insured wishes to use the rental car endorsement. Due to the error on behalf of the insurance agent in forgetting to add the coverage, the cost for the rental car could be claimed under the insurance agent's errors and omissions policy.

- **Garage Coverage Liability**: Liability coverage for auto-type businesses such as dealerships, service/gas stations, and valet services while they are engaged in servicing, repairing, cleaning, parking, and storing vehicles not owned by their business. Special classifications are given to autos, called **symbols**, when a business is in possession of vehicles they do not own. **Symbol 30** defines client's vehicles that are being repaired, serviced, cleaned, or stored for safekeeping. **Symbol 31** defines vehicles that are held for sale and includes physical damage coverage. Garage coverage liability does not cover the work that is being performed on any vehicles.

- **Liquor Liability**: Often referred to as "dramshop" coverage, which is the legal term in the United States for locations where alcoholic beverages are served. Liquor liability coverage is available to those whose business is the legal sale, distribution, and manufacturing of beverages containing alcohol. Covered perils, maximum limits, and exclusions vary, sometimes considerably, from state to state.

- **Product Guarantee Liability**: Insurance for claims against manufacturers, sellers, and leasers of products that have performance guarantees. Covered perils are very specific and define under what circumstances losses are covered, such as design deficiencies, defects, and warranty failures. These types of losses can be substantial, making this type of liability insurance one of the most expensive on the market.

- **Special Event Liability**: Provides liability coverage for individual events that take place over a course of a few hours to a few days. As long as the event is considered to be inclusive, meaning a continuation of the same event, one liability policy can cover the entire occasion. Venues where events take place often make this coverage mandatory. As part of the facility rental agreement, regardless of whether payment is being made for the rental of the space, venues are commonly added as an additional insured. Liquor liability and event cancellation are usually available as endorsements. Examples of special events include weddings, fundraisers, corporate seminars, music concerts, and business meetings. Claims under special event liability policies are oftentimes very diversified. For example, claims could incur if the lead singer cancels a concert due to severe laryngitis, stage curtains are damaged by fake blood being used as a prop in a theatre production, or a wedding guest has an anaphylactic reaction to a food substance at the reception.

Practice Questions

1. A customer falls through a broken step at a business and only realizes two months later that they have sustained a back injury that will require surgery and several weeks of missed work. The customer now reports the claim, but the commercial general liability (CGL) insurance policy for the business expired one month ago. Under which of the following policies could coverage be available to cover their injuries?
   a. Occurrence made policy
   b. Shrinking limit policy
   c. Uninsured business policy
   d. Claims made policy

2. Which of the following would ALWAYS be excluded from coverage on ALL insurance policies?
   a. Liquor liability, trademark violations, misappropriation of funds by the insured
   b. Government seizures, intentional acts, acts of terrorism
   c. Malpractice liability, criminal activity by the named insured, property that is being transported
   d. Product guarantee liability, employer's liability, criminal fines

3. An insured's personal automobile is vandalized, and the following items are stolen: cell phone, leather jacket, portable DVD player, spare tire, wool blankets, purse, chrome wheel covers, and factory installed GPS, radio/CD player, speakers, and DVD player. If the insured has physical damage coverage for comprehensive losses, which of the following will ALL be covered after the deductible is paid?
   a. Leather jacket, radio/CD player, purse, spare tire
   b. Speakers, chrome wheel covers, GPS, DVD player
   c. Cell phone, speakers, spare tire, leather jacket
   d. Purse, portable DVD player, chrome wheel covers, wool blankets

4. Commercial property policies include a "control of property condition", commonly known as CCC. What three words make up the CCC acronym?
   a. Care, conduct, custody
   b. Capacity, care, cargo
   c. Care, custody, control
   d. Control, cause, claim

5. Supplemental payments would NOT pay for which of the following?
   a. Loss of third party property
   b. Legal cost to investigate a claim
   c. Post judgment interest
   d. Emergency treatment

6. When a driver is unable to purchase mandatory liability insurance for their vehicle from insurance companies in their state due to their poor driving record, they can still purchase the liability insurance under what plan?
   a. Underinsured driver plan
   b. Assigned risk plan
   c. Uninsured motorist plan
   d. General liability plan

7. Widget Company employs leased, volunteer, and temporary workers for a few weeks every year. Which of the following statements is TRUE?

a. Volunteer workers are employees
b. Temporary and volunteer workers are employees
c. Temporary workers are employees
d. Leased workers are employees

8. If an insurance company voids a commercial property policy due to the insured's misrepresentation, what coverage will the insured have for losses and for how long?

a. There will be no coverage for any losses.
b. Coverage will be limited to 30 days.
c. There will be coverage until the expiry date.
d. Coverage expired on the day the misrepresentation was discovered.

9. Sally has a personal auto insurance policy that includes coverage for third party liability, medical payments, uninsured motorist, physical damage (both collision and comprehensive), and underinsured motorist. Sally is struck by a third party's vehicle while she is crossing the street. Which of the following statements is TRUE?

a. Sally could receive coverage under third party liability or uninsured motorist.
b. Sally could receive coverage under property damage, underinsured motorist, or medical payments.
c. Sally would receive no coverage under her personal auto insurance policy as she was not in the vehicle when the accident occurred.
d. Sally could receive coverage under uninsured motorist or medical payments.

10. Which of the following can ALL be found in the declaration section of an insurance policy?

a. Policy exclusions, coverage territory, other insurance condition, policy changes
b. Coverage summary, policy effective dates, premium amount, list of forms
c. Special provisions, limitations of liability, mortgagee clause, policy exclusions
d. Endorsements, liberalization, valuation clause, supplemental payments

11. ABC Construction uses a front end loader in their daily business. How is the front end loader classified on their commercial general liability (CGL) policy?

a. As an automobile
b. As an automobile while on a public road and as mobile equipment while it is used off public roads
c. As mobile equipment
d. As an auto and mobile equipment

12. "Dramshop" coverage is the industry term that covers liability for businesses who deal in which commodity?

a. Liquor
b. Garages
c. Advertising
d. Contracting

13. Joe is driving his insured personal automobile while working as a taxi driver. While taking a fare to their destination, Joe collides with a third party and is found at fault for the accident. The third party does not have insurance on his vehicle, but Joe has property damage (collision) coverage on his own insurance policy. How will Joe's damages be handled by his personal automobile insurer?

a. The insurer will pay Joe's damages under his uninsured motorist coverage.
b. The insurer will not cover the damages because Joe is at fault.
c. The insurer will cover Joe's damages under his collision coverage because the third party was not insured.
d. The insurer will not cover any of Joe's damages because he was using his personal automobile as a taxi at the time of the accident.

14. Which of the following claims is NOT excluded under a commercial general liability (CGL) policy owned by the insured?

a. An electrician, the insured, turns on a switch he just rewired and is injured by a power surge.
b. A plumber, the insured, is fixing a customer's sink and accidently forgets to shut off the water while they go to the store to purchase a part, and water damages their customer's property.
c. A store owner, the insured, leaves a portable heater running in the back room of their premises, and it melts several laptop computers owned by the insured.
d. A shop's employee, insured on the employer's CGL policy, trips over an extension cord at their place of business and breaks their ankle.

15. Errors and omissions liability is meant to cover which exposure?

a. Malpractice by a professional
b. Failure of a product guarantee
c. Environmental damages
d. Inadvertent third party economic losses

16. ABC Store is having a sale on the Widgets. A newspaper advertisement prints the sale price as being $1.99 instead of $19.99, an obvious printing error. ABC Store sells the 100 Widgets they have in stock for $1.99 and submits a claim to their advertising liability insurer for their loss. ($1999 - $199 = $1800). What coverage will there be for the $1800 loss due to the printing error?

a. There will be $1800 coverage minus any deductibles.
b. The insurance company will cover the $1800 loss, but they will subrogate against the newspaper responsible for the error for the $1800.
c. This is coverage for the $1800 for the 100 Widgets sold, but the insurer will not cover any "rain checks" given out by ABC Store for additional Widgets at the sale price of $1.99.
d. There is no coverage for the $1800 under advertising liability policies.

17. What coverage is afforded under the MCS90 endorsement that all motor carriers are required, by law, to have on their commercial automobile policy unless they can provide financial proof for self-insurance?

a. Bodily injury and property damage liability for third parties
b. Bodily injury liability and medical payments for third parties
c. Property damage liability and cargo insurance for third parties
d. Uninsured motorist and underinsured motorist liability for third parties

18. ABC Company has a crime insurance policy that covers theft by their employees that has been in force for two months. It is discovered today that an employee unlawfully took company products nine months ago. The employee quit three months ago. ABC Company's current policy was issued on a discovery basis. Will the loss be covered by the current crime insurance policy and why?
 a. Yes, because the policy is issued on a discovery basis.
 b. No, because the theft was discovered after the employee no longer worked there.
 c. Yes, because the employee is no longer employed at ABC Company.
 d. No, because the new crime insurance policy has only been in force for two months.

19. Jill has a personal automobile policy with a $500 deductible. Jill is at fault for an accident where John is injured. How will Jill's deductible apply in the claim settlement for John's injuries?
 a. Jill will pay a portion of the deductible depending on the amount of the settlement.
 b. Jill will pay the $500 deductible.
 c. Jill will not have to pay the deductible if her liability limit is $1,000,000 or higher.
 d. Jill will not pay any deductible.

20. Which of the following has necessitated the creation of cyber liability insurance?
 a. Confidentiality breaches
 b. Cyber crimes
 c. Electronic advertising
 d. Online policy purchases

21. How are workers' compensation insurance policies best defined?
 a. Discriminatory - Coverage for workers who are exposed to discrimination in the workplace
 b. Beneficiary - Benefits are provided by states that ensure beneficiaries of workers are compensated
 c. Disability - Coverage for workers who suffer disabilities
 d. Statutory - Individual states determine the laws concerning coverage and benefits

22. Jack is driving when an animal jumps from the ditch hitting the side of his car and causing damage. However, the animal runs off into the woods. What coverage under Jack's personal automobile insurance policy, if purchased, would cover the damage to Jack's car?
 a. Comprehension coverage
 b. Collision coverage
 c. Comprehensive coverage
 d. Collider coverage

23. Which liability insurance policy is designed to cover deficiencies in the amount of liability insurance on other policies owned by the insured?
 a. Umbrella liability
 b. Errors and omissions liability
 c. Special event liability
 d. Shelter liability

24. Which of the following demonstrates the liability limits of coverage when written as a split limit 250/500/150?

   a. 250,000 minimum bodily injury per person, 500,000 minimum bodily injury per occurrence, 150,000 minimum property damage per policy period
   b. 250,000 maximum bodily injury per person, 500,000 maximum bodily injury per occurrence, 150,000 maximum property damage per occurrence
   c. 250,000 maximum property damage, 500,000 maximum bodily injury per person, 150,000 maximum bodily injury per occurrence
   d. 250,000 maximum bodily injury, 500,000 maximum property damage, 150,000 maximum property damage per occurrence.

25. Under a commercial general liability policy, which of the following people can make a claim against the company for medical payments?

   a. Customer
   b. Employee
   c. Owner
   d. Maintenance staff

Answer Explanations

1. A: Occurrence made insurance policies allow for coverage as long as the loss occurred during the policy period, even if the claim is not reported until after the policy expired. There could be a statute of limitations, but it would be at least two years. Shrinking limit is a clause within an insurance policy that deducts an insured's legal expenses from the total liability limit. Claims made insurance policies state that claims must occur and be reported within the policy period. Uninsured business policy is not a valid answer.

2. B: Losses as a result of government seizures, intentional acts, and acts of terrorism are ALWAYS excluded from ALL insurance policies. Liquor liability, malpractice liability, property that is being transported, product guarantee liability, and employer's liability are all available for purchase but are not ALWAYS insured. Misappropriation of funds by the insured, criminal activity by the insured, and criminal fines coverage are not insurable.

3. B: Comprehensive coverage only covers theft of items that are permanent parts of the vehicle. Speakers, chrome wheel covers, GPS, and DVD player as well as the spare tire are all considered permanent parts of the vehicle. The insured's personal property insurance policy would cover the leather jacket, purse, cell phone, portable DVD player, and wool blankets. It is important to note that the "factory installed" DVD player would be covered. Since the other DVD player is listed as being "portable", it would be considered personal property.

4. C: Care, custody, and control make up the acronym CCC, the "control of property condition" in a commercial property policy. The other acronym definitions are not valid answers.

5. A: Loss of third party property would be covered under the liability portion of a policy. Supplemental payments cover legal costs to investigate claims, bond payments, emergency treatment, legal fees, lost earnings, prejudgment, and post judgment interest. Other supplemental payments could be covered but losses to a third party would not be.

6. B: Assigned risk plans allow drivers to purchase insurance from the state when they are ineligible to purchase mandatory liability insurance from an insurance company due to their driving or claims record. Underinsured driver plan, Uninsured motorist plan, and general liability plan are not valid answers.

7. D: Leased workers are classified as employees on a commercial general liability (CGL) policy. Volunteer and temporary workers are not classified as employees.

8. A: Since the insurance company voided the policy, no losses will be covered. While the insurance company may give the insured coverage for a limited time after misrepresentation is discovered, they have the option to void the policy so there will be no coverage. Voiding an insurance policy means the policy never existed.

9. D: Sally could be covered under the uninsured motorist or medical payments sections of her personal auto policy as the motorist who struck her could be uninsured and medical payments could cover her injuries. It is important to note the "or" in the sentence as Sally could not receive payments under both coverages for the same injury. This illustrates how only "one" word in the insurance industry can be very important. Sally could not receive coverage under her third-party liability as that covers bodily injury and property damage to third parties only. Her property damage coverage would not cover her injuries as it covers damage to her vehicle. Sally could have coverage for an underinsured motorist if the third party that hit her had a lower liability limit than she did. Sally is covered for losses under her personal auto insurance policy as long as the loss is vehicle related, even in the case of being struck by a third party's vehicle while her vehicle is parked in her garage.

10. B: The coverage summary, policy effective dates, premium amount, and list of forms can all be found in the declarations section of an insurance policy. While the other answer choices all contain different parts of an insurance policy, only those listed in Choice *B* are ALL included in the declarations section.

11. C: A front end loader is classed as mobile equipment because transportation is not the main use of this piece of equipment even though it may travel on main roads to get to a job site. Vehicles cannot be classed as an automobile and mobile equipment, it must be one or the other.

12. A: "Dramshop" is the legal term in the United States to describe establishments where liquor is served.

13. D: A vehicle insured on a personal automobile policy cannot be used for business purposes, so Joe's insurance company will not pay for his damages because he was using his vehicle as a taxi at the time of the accident.

14. B: A plumber, who is the insured, accidently caused damage to their customer's property which would be covered under the plumber's commercial general liability (CGL) policy. The electrician would not be covered because they are the insured and cannot claim an injury to themselves under his CGL policy. The store owner damaged their own laptop computers which is not covered under their CGL policy. The shop employee is excluded as employees of the insured are not covered under the CGL policy.

15. D: Errors and omissions liability policies cover inadvertent activities that result in losses to a third party. Malpractice by a professional, failure of a product guarantee, and environmental damages liability are other available liability policies that offer specific coverages.

16. D: Pricing errors are excluded from coverage under advertising liability insurance policies.

17. A: All motor carriers are required, by law, to have the MCS90 endorsement, unless they can prove financially able to be self-insured, that covers bodily injury and property damage liability to third parties.

18. A: ABC Company's crime insurance policy was issued on a discovery basis which means the theft by the employee will be covered because the theft was discovered while the current policy was in force. Coverage would not be determined on whether the employee was employed at the time of the theft discovery.

19. D: Jill will not pay any deductible. On personal automobile insurance policies, there are no deductibles for bodily injury or property damage claims by third parties. If the insured has physical damage coverage (collision and comprehensive), deductibles will apply.

20. B: Technological advances that have led to an increase in cyber crime have directly led to the creation of cyber liability insurance that covers losses by businesses relating to the use of computers. The other responses are not valid.

21. D: Workers' compensation insurance policies are statutory in nature meaning that individual states determine the laws concerning coverage and benefits. Discriminatory, beneficiary, and disability are not valid responses.

22. C: Comprehensive coverage would cover the damage because even though Jack "collided" with the animal, collision coverage covers Jack if he "collides" with an inanimate object. A car or guardrail is considered an inanimate object because it cannot run under its own power. An animal, however, is an 'animate' object, operating under its own power, so coverage would apply under comprehensive. "Comprehension" is a common mistake when insured's mean to say "comprehensive". Collider is not a valid coverage.

23. A: Umbrella liability policies will cover short falls in liability insurance policies owned by the insured and will "drop down" to supply additional liability insurance. Errors and omissions and special event liability policies are not umbrella liability policies. Shelter liability is not an insurance policy.

24. B: Liability reflected as the split limit 250/500/150 would be defined as 250,000 maximum bodily injury per person, 500,000 maximum bodily injury per occurrence, and 150,000 maximum property damage per occurrence.

25. A: Liability is for third-party claims. A customer who visits an insured's place of business and obtains a minor injury would file a claim under medical payments. Owners and employees of the company are not eligible to file claims under medical payments.

Casualty Insurance Terms and Related Concepts

Casualty Insurance

Universal Terminology and Clauses

Insurance policies contain uniform information that is common to all policy wordings. In addition, certain insurance policy types are regularly known in the industry as abbreviations. For example, a **Commercial General Liability** policy is referred to as **CGL**. Frequently abridged references are indicated in parentheses throughout this manual and the accompanying practice exam questions and answer key to assist you in becoming familiar with the terms. The following stipulations, provisions, and conditions can be found on all of the policies covered in this manual. Exceptions, if any, are noted in parentheses.

Insurance policies are divided into the following six sections:

- **Declarations:** Usually contained on the first page of an **insurance policy**, the **declarations** state the insured's name, address, mailing address and other contact information, policy effective dates, summary of coverages provided, premium amount, and a list of forms included in the policy package.

- **Insuring Agreements:** A summary of the coverage provided, showing more detail than the declarations page, coverage limits, restrictions, exclusions, endorsements and any special provisions. It is imperative that insureds read their entire policy package, as limitations of coverage can be listed anywhere in the policy.

- **Definitions:** Common terms contained in the insurance policy are listed, alphabetically, with brief definitions.

- **Exclusions:** Listed in this section, exclusions are expanded upon with more detailed information provided. Whether it is titled an all risk or named perils policy, or any variation thereof, an insurance policy will always have losses for which coverage is not included. Most losses not covered by the policy will be listed in the exclusions section of the policy package. It is important to remember that exclusions can be stated anywhere in the policy package.

- **Conditions:** Obligations of the insurer and the insured are listed in the conditions. These duties include the insured's requirement to report losses within a specified period of time, cooperating with the insurer during the reporting, investigating and settlement of claims and assisting the insurer to obtain required information. Insurers agree to cover insured losses that occur when the policy is in force.

- **Endorsements:** Any modifications to the insurance policy are called endorsements which are listed in detail in this section. Endorsements can add, exclude, or restrict coverages. For example, an endorsement can add coverage for theft committed by employees, exclude damage caused to a stand-alone sign by a tornado or set a limit on coverage for computer and software in the event of a loss.

Coverage Territory: The United States, Canada, including their territories and possessions, make up the **coverage territory** for claims arising from an insured peril. Injuries and damages incurred while travelling via waterways or in the air between the locations outlined as being in the coverage territory will be covered if they are caused by an insured peril. Injuries and damages that occur outside the coverage territory can be compensated for if the following conditions are met:

- The business made or sold the goods in the coverage territory.
- An insured person is away for a limited amount of time doing activities on behalf of the business, but they permanently reside in the coverage territory.
- Personal and advertising offences rising by way of electronic communication such as over the Internet.

Out of State Coverage Extension: This coverage increases the liability on an insured's auto policy to the minimum liability amount required, by law, when the insured is driving their auto in a state other than the state where they reside. For example, an insured lives in New York state where the minimum coverage is 25/50/10, which means 25,000 for bodily injury, 50,000 for all injuries, and 10,000 for property damage. The insured travels to North Carolina in their vehicle where the minimum coverage is 30/60/25, which means 30,000 for bodily injury, 60,000 for all injuries, and 25,000 for property damage. If the insured has an accident while traveling in North Carolina, their insurance policy will increase the liability coverage to 30/60/25, the minimum required in North Carolina.

Shrinking Limit: Commercial, or business, insurance policies covering liability may have a **shrinking limit** provision. Most commonly found on employment practices liability policies, if the insured incurs legal expenses during the claims process, the legal expenses will be deducted from the maximum coverage limit of the policy. After the legal expenses are deducted, the amount of coverage that is left will be used to settle the claim. For example, John Hancock is sued by a former employee for wrongful dismissal. Hancock's legal fees to defend the claim are $25,000, and the maximum liability coverage on their policy is $500,000. If a settlement is reached with the former employee, there will only be $475,000 available to pay the claim.

Mortgage or Lienholder Condition: When an insured's property is used as security on a loan, the lender, known as the mortgagee or lienholder has a vested interest in the property. If the lender is listed on the insurance policy, under the mortgage or lienholder condition, the insurer is required to notify the lender of any changes to the policy or losses that could affect the value of the property or in the event that the policy is cancelled. Mortgagees and lienholders can require, for example, specific coverage and maximum deductible amounts as a condition of their agreement with their client. Insurance companies issue policies based on what coverage, deductible, etc. the insured requests. Although the insurance company must notify any mortgagee or lienholder listed on the policy of changes that could affect their interest in the risk being insured, the contract is between the insurance company and the insured so they can only act on the direction of the insured.

Insurance Under Two Or More Coverages: When an insured purchases more than one insurance policy, they may create a situation where **coverage** is provided for a loss under **two or more** policies. When a loss occurs, the primary policy will pay for the loss up to their coverage limit. If there is not enough coverage to satisfy the claim settlement amount. The additional policies, defined as providing surplus coverage, will pay up to their coverage limits until the settlement amount is reached. If an insured purchases policies from the same insurance company that result in **two or more coverages,** the company will usually designate which policy is primary and which is surplus. As insured's purchase policies from different companies that result in **two or more coverages** for the same loss, the insurance companies may agree that the policy purchased first is primary. However, losses that are **insured under two or more coverages** often lead to litigation in an effort to establish primary and surplus policies.

Policy Exclusions: Every insurance policy contains exclusions, defined as occurrences resulting in losses for which no coverage is afforded. Policies named 'All Risk' and 'All Perils' are misleading. For these types of policies, unless a peril is declared to be exempt from coverage, the loss is insured. It is important to note that even though perils that are not covered are stated in the exclusions section of an insurance policy, it is possible for excluded coverages to be listed anywhere within the policy wording and/or package. The following perils are excluded from coverage in all insurance policies:

- Injuries that are intentional or anticipated
- Bodily injury that is otherwise covered under workers' compensation or similar coverage
- Damage from any acts of war (whether or not war has been declared), terrorism, insurrection, revolution, rebellion, military action (whether or not by a recognized government)
- Nuclear losses such as radioactive, contamination, nuclear reaction, or radiation
- Losses resulting from legal government seizure
- Losses incurred as the result of, or in the committing of, any criminal activity by the insured (Liability insurance is available for some types of crimes when committed, for example, by an employee of a business)
- Any damage that is due to usual wear and tear

Subrogation: The process used for an insurance company to recoup money they have paid to cover damages for their insured when a third party is at fault for the loss is termed **subrogation**. Policy provisions state that when there is a loss, the insurance company retains the right to subrogate against any third party who is at fault for a loss, thus the insured transfers any subrogation rights. Policy wording may substitute the term subrogation with a clause stating, "**Our Right To Recover Payment**". Subrogation is most often used when there is a dispute over whom is at fault for a loss. In order for their insured not to be without their vehicle while liability is being decided, the insurance company will pay for their insured's losses, provided they are as a result of an insured peril and coverage was valid at the time of the loss, and be reimbursed by the third party, or their insurer, if they are found to be at fault, using the subrogation clause. Subrogation is also referred to as "transfer of rights" in some insurance policy wordings, meaning that the insured "transfers the right" from the insured to the insurer to subrogate against the third party.

Valuation Clause: In the insurance policy wording it will be cited what methods and calculations will be used by the insurer to determine the amount that will be paid in the event of a loss. Defined as the **valuation clause**, different formulas may be used depending on the loss and the type of insurance being used to pay the claim (liability, bodily injury, property damage). Valuation clauses may also state how the following losses will be calculated:

- Money (the face value of the money)
- Foreign Currency (equivalent United States value on the date of the loss)
- Securities (value on the date of the loss)

Actual Cash Value (ACV), Replacement, Repair, and Bodily Injury Compensation: Insurance companies use a variety of formulas for calculating damages in the event of a loss to the insured or a third party. These formulas will vary between insurance companies but there are some general calculations that are common. **Actual cash value** is defined as the fair market value of property, meaning what it would cost to purchase the property in the condition it was in at the time of the loss. Actual cash value is determined by calculating the current replacement cost of the property minus any **depreciation**. Insurance companies may also employ the **broad evidence rule** when determining actual cash value which takes into account factors such as the age and condition of the property at the time of the loss in addition to its tax value, the price of similar items on the market, and the original purchase price. For example, a television is a total loss and was purchased for $500 five years ago. Allowing for depreciation of $50 per year (minus $250), plus taking into account that the television was in perfect condition (plus $75), the actual cash value would be calculated as $325 ($500 - $250 + $75 = $325).

Replacement cost is the cost to replace the property with an item that is as close as possible to the one that was lost. Replacement cost insurance will often exceed the original price paid for the property, making this type of insurance more expensive. For example, a television cost $500 five years ago. In order to replace the television with one of the same size and quality could cost $650 in today's market. Insurance companies will repair property whenever it is feasible to do so as long as repairing the property will restore it to the same condition it was in before the loss. A constructive total loss occurs when the damage is so extensive that the cost for repairs would exceed the current value. This is often the case with vehicles and insurance companies will offer the insured the actual cash value of the vehicle as opposed to repairing the damage. When a loss is settled using actual cash value, the insured is often given the calculated amount for the property, with it being their option whether or not to replace the property. When a loss is settled for the replacement value, the insured will be obligated to replace the property.

Insurance policies will state how disputes between the insurer and the insured over the value of property will be settled. Most times, they will agree to each have their own adjuster calculate the value of the loss and be bound by the average between the two calculations. There are no common formulas for calculating **bodily injury** settlements. Insurance companies take into account a number of factors when determining the amount of settlements, including medical expenses, lost earnings, future lost income, future medical and rehabilitation expenses, long term care, emotional and physical pain and suffering, lifestyle changes and temporary or permanent disability or disfigurement. Often bodily injury claims take many months, or even years, to reach a settlement amount. There can be limitation amounts put on specific losses and policies can have different valuation clauses that will be used in determining the amount a loss is worth.

Supplemental payments are expenses paid by the insurance company, over and above the limit of insurance, in order to facilitate the investigation, defense, and settlement of claims. For example, if the liability limit on a personal auto insurance policy was $1,000,000, and the insurance company incurred costs of $8,500 under expenses defined as supplemental payments, the maximum amount of liability insurance would still be $1,000,000. There are sometimes limits to the amount that supplemental payments will cover. For example, when the insured misses a day of work in order to appear in court at the request of the insurance company, the company may only pay up to $250 for the wages lost. Costs incurred by the insured are deducted from the policy liability limit.

Employment Practice Liability policies are unique in that the defense supplemental payments include costs to cover the following:

- **Bond Payments:** Only bonds stated in the policy wording and directly related to the claim will be paid
- **Emergency Treatment:** Payments to cover emergency treatment for those involved during and directly after a claim has occurred
- **Investigation Costs:** Costs associated with investigating claims, for example, fees to obtain surveillance video
- **Legal Fees:** Lawyer, paralegal, legal assistant fees, etc. as they relate to a claim
- **Loss of Earnings:** When an insured is required to be away from their place of employment by the request of the insured, their lost wages can be covered
- **Prejudgment Interest:** Interest earned by judgment funds between the time the judgment is rendered and the time it is registered with the court, as long as the interest is not accounted for in the claim settlement
- **Post judgment Interest:** Interest earned by judgment funds between the time the judgment is registered with the court and the time it is paid to the third party, as long as the interest is not accounted for in the claim settlement

Post Loss Duties (Insured): Following a loss, or in the event of a potential claim, the insured is compelled to perform the following **post loss duties**:

- Promptly advise the insurance company of the loss or potential claim and provide details pertaining to the same.
- If possible, take steps to further prevent loss or damage. (For example, if a customer trips on a loose stair tread, whether or not they sustain bodily injury, the insured would be responsible to fix the tread before another mishap can occur.)
- Keep accurate notes of all details related to the loss and provide documents, records, etc., as requested by the insurer.
- Assist the insurance company, when asked, with investigating, defending, and settling claims.
- Notify the proper authorities, such as the police, if the situation warrants (for example, in the event of a burglary of the insured's home).

- Provide a proof of loss statement to the insurance company, when requested to do so.
- Permit the insurance company to appraise any damage before any property is repaired or disposed of.

Pro-Rata Versus Short Rate Refund: Upon an insured's request to cancel their policy before the expiration date, insurance companies use two methods to calculate how much returned, or unearned, premium the insured will receive. Refunds calculated on a **pro-rata** basis will receive more of a refund, if applicable, than refunds calculated on a **short rate** basis. Insurance companies use the short rate calculation as a deterrent, penalizing insured's who cancel a policy before the expiration date. Calculations vary among insurance companies as well as the decision whether or not to cancel a policy via short rate or pro rata.

Bankruptcy/Insolvency (Insured): In the event of **bankruptcy** or **insolvency** on the part of the insured, the insurer is still obligated to fulfill the terms under the insurance contract.

Underinsured Motorist Coverage (UIM or UIMBI): There is an important difference between uninsured and underinsured motorists. **Uninsured motorists** have no valid insurance at the time of a loss. **Underinsured motorists** have valid insurance; however, due to the maximum payout amounts stated on their insurance policy, they are considered to have insufficient insurance. State statues most often require a minimum amount of auto liability insurance to be purchased, but insureds may select higher limits. For example, the minimum amount of liability is set at $200,000 by the state, but the insured opts to buy $1,000,000 in liability for a higher premium. Coverage for underinsured motorists is not standard. There may be a minimum amount of coverage legislated by the state, an option to purchase underinsured motorist coverage at an additional premium, or it may be included in the policy premium. In order for uninsured motorist coverage to apply, in the event of a loss, the claimant must have a liability limit higher than that of the third party, and the third party must be at fault for the loss. For example, Joe is injured in an auto accident, and Bill is at fault. Joe has $1,000,000 liability on his policy while Bill has the state mandated minimum of $200,000. Joe's claim is settled for $500,000. If Joe has underinsured motorist coverage, Bill's liability will pay up to his policy limit of $200,000, and Joe's insurance will pay the remaining $300,000.

Assigned Risk Plan - Mandatory Auto Insurance: When a driver does not qualify to be insured by any insurance company operating in a state due to the driver's moving violations or claims history but is bound by law to have auto insurance to legally operate their vehicle, they can be offered coverage under an **assigned risk plan**. This is an insurance policy offered by the state government and usually administered by the Department of Motor Vehicles. All of the insurance companies selling automobile policies in the state pay a premium to the state's government who, in turn, have insurance policies available for high risk drivers. Premiums for assigned risk plans are significantly higher than for drivers who qualify for coverage with insurance companies. For example, a driver insured under the assigned risk plan as a consequence of having received 3 speeding tickets, a ticket for failing to wear their seatbelt, a 6 month license suspension, and an at fault accident within the past 6 years would pay a considerably higher premium than a driver with one at fault accident during the same time period. The difference can often be in the thousands of dollars.

Assigned Risk Plan - Workers' compensation: States may also offer assigned risk plans for businesses who do not qualify for usual **workers' compensation** policies. Again, the premiums are notably much higher than workers' compensation policies available from insurance companies operating in the state.

Companies with employees who routinely work in hazardous conditions that create much higher than normal possibilities or instances where substantial losses can occur often have to use this type of policy. For example, roofing contracts tend to have a history of frequent claims and will likely only find workers' compensation coverage under an assigned risk plan.

Named Insureds: Under the declaration section of a commercial general liability policy, persons considered to be **named insureds** are listed. Usually, only the owner of the policy is reflected by name. Persons fitting within the following descriptions, though not listed by name, are named insured's:

- Sole Proprietorship: Includes the insured owner of the policy and their legal partner
- Partnership/Joint Venture: Partners and members in addition to their legal partners
- Limited Liability Company (LLC): Managers and members
- Trust: Trustees
- Organization Not Listed Above: Stockholders, directors, and officers

In addition to the **named insureds**, the following are also insured when they are participating in business related activities:

- Volunteers
- Real estate manager
- Persons or legal representatives (for example, executor, lawyer) assuming the named insured's and policy owner's business after their incapacitation or death
- Employees of the insured not otherwise covered
- Organizations acquired by the policy owner (excluding partnerships, joint ventures, and limited liability companies) if the insured owns the majority of the organization. Coverage is limited to 90 days or until the current policy expires, whichever is earlier, and the organization must not have coverage elsewhere. Excludes all losses that occurred before the insured gained majority ownership.
- Individuals who transport the insured's property on a public road, provided they have the insured's consent

Your Right To Claim and Occurrence Information Condition: Applicable only to the claims-made form, the insurer will provide the following to the insured, covering the preceding 36 months:

- Any occurrences reported to the insurer
- Monies that have been placed in reserve and collected under both the general and products-completed operations aggregate limits

When the following apply, the insurer must provide the above information:

- Within 60 days of the policy expiration date, if the first named insured provides a written request. The insurer has 45 days to comply.
- 30 days before policy expiration date if the insurer is not offering renewal or if the policy is cancelled.

Pollution Liability Coverage Extension Endorsement: Provides bodily injury and property damage coverage but excludes clean-up costs.

Pollution Liability Coverage Form: Covers bodily injury and property damage caused by pollutants and including clean-up costs. This coverage is only available on a claims-made policy.

Liquor Liability Coverage Form: Provides liability coverage for those in the liquor business.

Owners and Contractors Protective Liability Coverage Form: Covers liability for those acting as independent contractors.

Casualty Insurance Basic Principles and Terminology

Casualty insurance is also called **liability insurance** or **third-party insurance**. In property insurance, there are two parties—the insurer and the insured. In casualty insurance, there are three parties—the insurer, the insured, and the third party. The third party is the **claimant**. The third party is entitled to receive compensation for covered losses. A **covered loss** is a loss that is covered by an insured peril on the policy, not caused intentionally and not criminal in nature.

Casualty insurance is defined as the legal liability of an insured or **additional insured**—a person or entity that is covered by an endorsement—when the insured inadvertently causes damage or injury to a third-party claimant.

Liability insurance covers accidents and occurrences. **Accidents** are events that are unforeseen, unintentional, or unexpected, and result in damage or loss. **Occurrences** are accidents or events that occur during the policy period, including events where there was exposure to certain conditions on an on-going basis.

Casualty insurance is an element of most insurance policies, but it can also be purchased as a stand-alone policy. Such is the case with an **umbrella policy**, which increases the amount of casualty insurance the insured has. An example would be an insured who has a personal property policy with an endorsement that covers an in-home business and a personal auto policy, each having $1,000,000 coverage included to cover casualty insurance losses. The insured could purchase an umbrella policy which increases his or her casualty insurance limit to $2,000,000 for both the personal property policy with the in-home business endorsement and the personal auto policy.

Tort Claims

A **tort claim** is filed by a third party who was injured or sustained damage by an insured party. The third party is entitled to reasonable financial compensation for his or her losses. Tort claims can be intentional or unintentional. **Intentional torts** cover a wide range of possibilities, not all of which can or will be compensated for under an insurance policy. For example, if a person punches another person in the face, he or she intentionally meant to cause harm to that person, and there is a generally known reasonable expectation that a punch to the face would result in injury, making the action an intentional tort. In that particular instance, the third party who was injured by being punched in the face would unlikely be successful in recouping damages for injuries under the insurance policy of the person who punched them.

Unintentional torts may be eligible for compensation for the third party. In another example, if a person jumped in front of a third party, meaning simply to scare him or her, and the third party suffered a heart attack as a result of the surprise, this would be considered an unintentional tort as the person did not intend to cause harm to the third party. In that particular instance, the third party may be able to recoup compensation for the injury as the act by the insured was unintentional.

Liability and Damage Classifications

Vicarious liability extends liability to an individual who has responsibility for another person or animal. It includes a parent's responsibility for a child or an employer's responsibility for employees. For example, if a minor child of an insured breaks a neighbor's window, the neighbor may receive compensation under the insurance policy owned by the insured, the parent of the minor child.

Absolute and strict liability losses occur when the insured is liable for damages to a third party, even in the absence of direct negligence. This type of liability refers to injury or damages that occur because of potentially dangerous activities or actions. For example, if an insured owns a venomous snake—even if precautions are taken to avoid injury to a third party, such as keeping the snake contained in a proper enclosure—the possibility still exists that a third party could be injured, which would constitute **absolute liability**. An example of **strict liability** would apply if a manufacturer's product were to cause injury to a consumer, such as a battery in a mobile device catching fire.

Several types of damages can be recouped by a third party to compensate for a loss. **Compensatory damages** are divided into general damages and special damages. **General damages** are awarded for losses that include pain and suffering, loss of physical or mental capacity or enjoyment of life, emotional distress, defamation, physical disfigurement, or loss of consortium—the loss of a family member/loved one or the diminished capacity of a family member/loved one.

Special damages are damages that can be calculated to compensate the third party for a quantifiable monetary loss and include damage to real or personal property, loss of earnings/wages, and medical expenses. **Punitive damages**, also referred to as **exemplary damages**, are awarded for losses that include acts that harmed the third party, such as defamation of character. Punitive damages benefit the third party financially but are also awarded as a means of deterring the person(s) who caused the damage from repeating the behavior in the future.

Speculative damages are compensation for damages that have not yet occurred. It is difficult to prove and calculate speculative damages, so this type of compensation is rarely paid. For example, if a third party had his or her reputation damaged by defamation and stated they would lose future economic business due to the defamation, it would be difficult to calculate the amount of future business the third party may or may not lose. **Nominal damages** can be awarded when damages can be proven to have harmed the third party but to a very nominal amount or when the third party cannot provide verifiable proof of the damages. When nominal damages are awarded, it is based more on principle than actual financial loss. An example would be a third party insisting that he or she was injured due to the negligence of the insured, but he or she provides no proof of the injury, such as medical records. The third party may be awarded $1.00 in damages, thus making the injury the fault of the insured.

Certificate of Insurance, Representations and Warranties

Certificate of Insurance

The **certificate of insurance** is a policy issued to an insured that states specific information, such as the policy-effective dates, the amount of coverage, and the insured perils. This document can be used as evidence of coverage for the insured. For example, following an automobile accident, the insured can present their certificate of insurance to a police officer as confirmation of coverage.

Representations

When filling out an application for insurance, the answers given by the applicant are called **representations**. It is imperative that applicants provide accurate information, as not doing so could lead to the policy being null and void, or cancelled for **misrepresentation.** For example, if the insured is asked whether there is a woodstove being used in the house and states there is not, the insurance company could deny the claim if there is a subsequent loss caused by the woodstove. Alternatively, if the insurance company discovers a woodstove in use on the insured's premises, the insurance company could elect to null and void or cancel the property-insurance policy, even absent of any loss occurring specific to the woodstove.

There is an important distinction between an insurance policy being null and void or cancelled by the insurer. When an insurer declares an insurance policy to be null and void, it means the insurance policy is treated as never having been issued or in effect. When an insurer elects to cancel an insurance policy, a specific cancellation date is given. When a policy is considered to be null and void, no coverage would be available for any losses. When an insurer cancels an insurance policy, there is coverage for losses from the inception date of the policy until the cancellation date stated by the insurer.

Warranties

Warranties are proclamations within an insurance policy that both the insured and the insurance company promise to abide by. If a warranty is breached, the entire policy can become null and void. For example, a business agrees never to store certain flammable products on their premises. If, part way through the policy period, the insured has a fire loss and the cause is determined to be a flammable product stored on the property, the insurance company could deny paying for the claim. In actual fact, the insurance company can null and void the policy, even in the absence of a claim being filed.

Risks/Losses

A **risk** is an exposure to loss that may or may not occur. Insurance policies provide coverage for some risks while others are excluded. Risks that are covered must be random and not guaranteed. For example, a lightning strike that causes a fire is random; therefore, the resulting damage is covered. However, a fire that is deliberately started by the insured is guaranteed to cause damage and therefore is not covered. Insurance companies evaluate risks using several different criteria and base the premium they charge on their findings. There are several ways that risks can be managed:

- **Risk avoidance** is accomplished by instituting measures that prevent the risk from occurring. For example, a construction company shuts down a work site for a day because the heavy rain in the forecast could result in an employee getting injured.
- When measures are implemented that decrease the probability that a loss will occur, it is called **risk reduction**. For example, having a chimney cleaned on a yearly basis will lessen the likelihood of a chimney fire.

- If someone does not want to take responsibility for certain risks, they can pass them over to someone else who is willing to take on the burden. Insurance policies provide a **transference of risk**. For example, a property owner does not want to pay for damage caused by a fire so they purchase an insurance policy to cover that risk for them.

- When someone agrees to be obligated to take on some or all of the risk themselves, they are practicing **risk retention.** Insurance policies usually have a dollar amount, or deductible, that must be paid by the insured before the insurance company will pay the balance of the claim. The insured is retaining some portion of the risk via the deductible; the higher the deductible, the lower the premium.

In order for a risk to be insured, the following conditions usually need to be met:

- The risk must be fortuitous, meaning that it has to have occurred due to chance as opposed to deliberately being caused by the insured. For example, if a vehicle were vandalized, the damage would be covered as long as the insured did not vandalize his or her own vehicle.

- The risk must not be catastrophic, meaning the risk is so large that the insurance company cannot feasibly pay for the loss. In order to safeguard against cataclysmic claims that would financially cripple an insurance company, the insurance company itself purchases protection, known as reinsurance. For example, an insured requests an excess liability policy, which is also known as an umbrella policy, with a limit of $25 million dollars. According to Insurance Company A's actuarial data, it knows that the insured is financially strong enough to pay a claim in the amount of $5 million dollars, but a $25 million claim would be a financial strain. Insurance Company A agrees to offer the insured an umbrella policy with a $25 million dollar limit, themselves insuring the insured up to $5 million dollars with an additional $20 million dollars of excess liability purchased from Insurance Company B. The insured now gets the full $25 million of liability that is needed, and Insurance Company A is protected for an unlikely, catastrophic claim.

- Premiums charged by an insurance company, in addition to earnings made from their investments, must allow them to pay for their incurred **losses** and **operating costs**, while still having a reasonable amount left over to allow for profit. It is vitally important that insurance companies accurately estimate their risks, as they must have enough funds invested in guaranteed securities to cover the claims they will be obligated to cover.

- Insurable risks must be definite in that the insurance company can ascertain the day and time the loss occurred, where the loss happened, and what caused the loss. These components are necessary for the insurance company to confirm if coverage was in place at the time of the loss and if the loss was the result of a covered peril.

- Policyholders must have an insurable interest in what is being insured and directly suffer from hardship in the event of a loss. Allowing insured persons to purchase insurance when they have no insurable interest would greatly increase claims, as the insured would stand to gain from any claim that occurred. For example, if the insurance is covering a property, the insured must suffer a financial loss if fire destroys the property.

- Risks covered by an insurance policy must be calculated using the law of large numbers. Insurance companies gather as much information as possible about risks so they can accurately predict their risk exposure and determine what premium to charge. Insurance companies must take into account data garnered from a large demographic in order to assure accuracy. For example, the insurance company would look at the history of weather-related losses in an entire state as opposed to weather-related losses on one street.

- Only **pure risk** can be insured. **Speculative risks** are not eligible for coverage. Pure risk always results in a loss. Speculative risk can result in a loss or a gain. For example, fire is a pure risk as the outcome will always be a loss. Gambling is an example of speculative risk as it could lead to a loss or a gain. Therefore, insurance against fire damage can be purchased while insurance to cover gambling losses cannot be purchased.

- There must be a risk of significant loss to the insured. Insurance companies will not provide policies where the cost to settle a claim would be more than the value of the loss. For example, if a regular pen were the only item insured and it was stolen, the insurance company would pay out more in expenses to cover the claim than the cost to replace the pen.

- Rates charged by insurance companies must be fair in that average consumers can afford the policy premium. Insurance companies cannot charge such a high premium that they would lose very little in the event of a claim. For example, if an insurance policy with a limit of $1,000,000 costs $900,000 in premium, the cost for the policy is unreasonable.

- The probability of loss and the attendant cost must be calculable. These two elements define the calculable loss. Probability of loss is determined using a number of factors to predict various risks. Attendant cost is the reasonable estimation of the value that can be recovered as the result of a claim.

Negligence

Negligence occurs when an act is unintentional but causes a loss to a third party, such as property damage or bodily injury. An insurance policy will reimburse damages to the third party if the insured inadvertently caused a loss to occur, and the loss is covered by the insurance policy. Losses suffered by a third party are covered under the liability portion of the insurance policy. In order for an insured to be held negligent, or at fault, for the loss, the third party must prove their culpability. When attempting to prove negligence, several factors must apply.

- The legal burden to have prevented the loss from occurring must rest on the insured. For example, say the insured transported a three-year-old child in their vehicle and did not use a car seat. If the child were injured, the insured would be held negligent, as the insured should have known it was illegal to transport a three-year-old child in a vehicle without the proper restraints.

- The insured's actions must be the **proximate**, or direct, cause of the damage—meaning the damage is attributed to the fault of the insured. For example, if an insured runs a red light and collides with another vehicle, the insured's action of running the red light is the proximate cause of the loss.

- There must be measurable damage or injury to the third party. For example, if a third party claims they fell on the insured's property but can produce no evidence of injuries or witnesses to their fall, the purported damage to the third party cannot be calculated.

- Proper precautions must have been neglected by the insured to avoid the loss, and the insured must have been obligated to provide a standard of care. For example, an insured knows their front steps are unsafe, but they do not take measures to either fix the stairs or sufficiently warn others not to use them. If a third party is injured during the course of using the stairs, the insured can be found negligent for the third party's injuries.

Comparative negligence occurs when both parties are found at fault for a portion of the loss. When recovering damages, the third party will only be able to collect the percentage of the amount attributed to the insured. For example, say the insured is found 75% at fault for the injuries sustained by the third party in a car accident. Due to the fact that the third party was not wearing a seatbelt, as required by law, the third party is found to be 25% at fault for the injuries they suffered. The insurance company would contend that the injuries suffered by the third party would have been less severe had the third party been wearing their seatbelt. The third party would only be able to recoup 75% of the damages awarded.

When a third party is found partially at fault for a loss, under **contributory negligence,** the third party is not entitled to recover any damages. It does not matter what percentage of the loss is attributed to the third party. For example, a pedestrian, defined as the third party, is hit by a vehicle while crossing the street, and they are deemed 50% responsible for their own injuries because they were not in a designated crosswalk. Under contributory negligence, the pedestrian could not collect any damages.

Insureds may utilize these defenses when accused of negligence by a third party:

- Contributory negligence

- Comparative negligence

- **Assumption of risk** is assumed when the risk should have been obvious to the third party. In very simplified terms, if the third party sees that a roller coaster has two loops and steep drops, they cannot blame the ride operator if they get a stomachache.

- **Last clear chance** happens when the third party clearly had the chance to avoid the loss but failed to do so. For example, an insured has adequately blocked off a set of stairs that are obviously broken and, therefore, unsafe. In addition, the insured gives the third party a verbal warning not to use the stairs. If the third party ignores all warnings and uses the stairs, which leads to injury, they cannot say the insured is negligent for the injuries they sustained.

- **Intervening clause** pertains to an event that could not have been controlled by the insured and causes additional damage or injury to a third party. For example, say the insured hits a pedestrian with a vehicle. When the pedestrian, defined as the third party, is being transferred to the hospital, the paramedics drop the gurney, causing further injury to the pedestrian. The intervening clause states that the additional injuries will be covered, because the insured had no way to prevent the paramedics from dropping the pedestrian.

When proven to be liable for losses suffered by a third party, general and special damages can be awarded. **General damages** cover physical losses such as pain and suffering and decreased quality of life. **Special damages** cover fixed losses such as hospital bills and replacement of property.

Insurance Policy Standards

Principle of Indemnity and Aleatory Contract

All forms of insurance are based on a fundamental purpose, which is called the **principle of indemnity**. When a loss occurs, the insurance company will compensate the insured for the loss they incurred up to the policy limit. The purpose of the insurance policy is to restore the insured to the same position they were in prior to the loss. However, the insured cannot profit from the loss. For example, the insured owns what would be considered a standard, one-level ranch house with the usual household contents. The house and contents are completely destroyed by fire. Under the insured's policy, fire is an insured peril, and the insured is entitled to the replacement of their house and contents. The insurance company would build a house and replace the contents to resemble as closely as possible the house and contents that were destroyed by the fire. However, the insured would not be eligible to have a two-story house that is twice the size of the house they lost, with gold plated fixtures, and a Renoir in the living room.

Insurance policies are a type of **aleatory contract**, where the amount paid by either party is unequal. For example, an insured may pay premiums for many years and never have a claim, or they may have one claim that amounts to much more than the total premiums they have paid.

Sources Used to Analyze Risk Exposure

Insurance companies employ underwriters who use information supplied by various sources to minimize the company's risk. Since insurance companies are in business to make a profit, they have to collect more premiums and receive more income from their investments than they pay out in claims. Data and statistical analytics such as economic forecasts, highway safety test results, crime reports, environmental studies, and industry trends are examples of the material used to analyze risk exposure and calculate insurance premiums. Underwriters pay close attention to the data in order to avoid things like adverse selection. For example, if an area has often been besieged by storms that produce hail the size of golf balls over the past few years, the insurance company could suffer major losses if they have a high volume of insurance policies in that area covering losses due to hail. Having analyzed things like weather data and claims experience, insurance companies may choose to limit the amount of policies they sell in that geographical area, exclude damage caused by hail as an insured peril, or increase the deductible that is payable by the insured as a means of limiting the amount of claims they will have to cover. It is imperative that underwriters follow the Fair Credit Reporting Act, as they deal with personal and sensitive information in the course of their work.

Approval Requirements to Change Forms and Rates

Insurance companies require their state's approval when making changes to their forms and rates. The following are methods used by the state's insurance departments to grant approval.

- **Prior Approval:** Changes must be approved by the state before they can be used.
- **Flex Rating:** Changes only require approval if they exceed a certain percentage.

- **File and Use:** Changes come into effect upon filing, but the state retains the right to cancel or modify the changes.
- **Open Competition Rating:** Insurance companies can set their own rates, as the state believes there are enough insurance companies operating in their state to keep the rates competitive without state intervention.
- **Mandatory State:** Insurance companies must abide by the rates set by the state.

Practice Questions

1. Which of the following would NOT be used to analyze risk exposures?
   a. Historical weather data
   b. Crime reports
   c. The number of insurance companies operating in the state
   d. Highway safety tests

2. For an insured to be found negligent for a third party's injuries, which of the following does NOT need to be proven?
   a. The insured was obligated to provide a standard of care.
   b. The insured's actions were the proximate cause of the loss.
   c. The insured was present when the loss occurred.
   d. There was a legal burden on the insured.

3. An insured could purchase and own which of the following policies because they have an insurable interest?
   a. A personal auto policy on the insured's brother's car if the brother has no license
   b. A property policy on the insured's mother as the insured is her beneficiary
   c. A commercial liability policy for the company where the insured is employed
   d. A property policy on a house owned by the insured and their spouse

4. A third party is found to be 25% at fault for their own injuries, and the insured is found to be 75% at fault; however, the third party will receive no compensation. This is defined as what type of negligence?
   a. Comparative
   b. Gross
   c. Contributory
   d. Criminal

5. An insurance company discovers that the insured, when asked, did NOT disclose the two DUI's they incurred two-and-a-half years ago while completing an application for an auto-insurance policy. Due to the insured's misrepresentation, what option is available to the insurance company?
   a. Require the insured to sign an affidavit promising not to drive while intoxicated
   b. Insist the insured provide proof that their fines have been paid
   c. Have the insured criminally charged for nondisclosure
   d. Null and void the insurance contract

6. Which two items need to be calculable in order for a risk to be insured?
   a. Probability of loss and attendant cost
   b. Premium charge and amount of profit
   c. Amount paid per loss and maximum liability limit
   d. Number of claims versus loss ratio

7. Insurance companies retain the right to recover the damages they paid when a third party is at fault for a loss in a process known as what?
   a. Subrogation
   b. Reimbursement
   c. Supplemental coverage
   d. Waiving the deductible

8. Which of the following is NOT a method state insurance boards use to grant rate changes?
   a. File and use
   b. Flex rating
   c. Prior approval
   d. Percentage state

9. An insured borrows a neighbor's ride-on lawn mower. While the insured is operating the mower, a rock is propelled from under the mower and spewed across the lawn. It hits a third party, causing injury. Which answer describes if, or how, the loss will be covered, under the insured's personal auto policy?
   a. Cover the third party's injuries under the casualty section
   b. Provide no coverage
   c. Cover the third party's injuries under the uninsured motorist section
   d. Provide coverage, but only to the bodily-injury limit stated on the policy

10. Which of the following is NOT eligible to be paid under supplemental coverage?
   a. Bail bond if the insured is arrested for property damage
   b. Claim-investigation costs
   c. Loss of earnings by the insured
   d. Prejudgment and post judgment interest

11. Which occurrence could prompt the insurance company to use their reinsurance policy to pay for losses?
   a. Property damage and injury results when a mechanical breakdown causes a vehicle to plunge into a lake.
   b. A fire at the insured's property is proven to be arson.
   c. A tornado destroys 100 homes insured by the insurance company.
   d. Bodily injury is incurred when a bus hits two pedestrians.

12. Which of the following is true of supplementary payments?
   a. Paid by the insurance company to cover the costs of investigating, defending, and settling claims
   b. Always deducted from the policy's liability limit
   c. Designed to never have a limit on any specific expenses
   d. Paid by the third party

13. What type of risk is defined when the insured has to pay a deductible on all claims?
   a. Risk retention
   b. Transference of risk
   c. Risk avoidance
   d. Risk reduction

14. Insurance policies are which type of product (meaning the amount paid by either party is unequal)?
   a. Aleatory
   b. Exposure
   c. Liability
   d. Premium

15. Insurance policies do NOT cover speculative risks. Only pure risks can be covered. Which of the following is defined as a speculative risk?
   a. Vandalism
   b. Fire
   c. Stock market securities
   d. Water damage

16. Where, specifically, can an insurer list coverage exclusions in an insurance policy wording?
   a. Only under the declaration and exclusion sections
   b. Only under the exclusions section
   c. Anywhere in the policy wording
   d. Only under the coverage and exclusion sections

17. An insured's vehicle is in an accident that is the fault of a third party. If the insured's insurance company pays for the damage to their own insured's vehicle and then recoups the money they paid from the third party, what term describes this process?
   a. Valuation
   b. Subrogation
   c. Misrepresentation
   d. Liberalization

18. Jack has purchased the underinsured motorist coverage option on his personal automobile insurance policy. Jack is injured in an accident where the third party is at fault. How will the underinsured motorist coverage affect Jack's claim for bodily injury?
   a. If Jack's liability limit is $1,000,000 and the third party's liability limit is $1,000,000, Jack's liability limit will increase to $2,000,000.
   b. If Jack's liability limit is $1,000,000 and the third party's liability limit is $500,000, Jack's liability limit will increase to $1,000,000.
   c. If Jack's liability limit is $1,000,000 and the third party's liability limit is $500,000, Jack's liability limit will decrease to $500,000.
   d. If Jack's liability limit is $1,000,000 and the third party's liability limit is $200,000, Jack's liability limit will decrease to $800,000.

19. Which of the following is NOT required for an insured to do in the event that they are advised of a claim against their insurance policy as a condition of the post loss duties?
   a. Take necessary action, if able to, that will prevent further loss
   b. Provide a proof of loss statement to the insurance company when requested
   c. Get two separate estimates on the cost of the damage
   d. Notify the insurance company as soon as possible about the claim

20. An insured cancels their policy mid-term. Which of the following refund calculations will result in the insured getting the largest refund of any unearned premium?
   a. Short rate calculation
   b. Rebate clause calculation
   c. Pro-rata calculation
   d. Penalty calculation

21. An insured has a liability policy that has a shrinking limit provision. Which of the following demonstrates shrinking limit in the event where the insured is sued by a third party?
   a. The shrinking limit provision states that the insured will be responsible for their own legal expenses.
   b. Due to the shrinking limit provision, the insured's legal expenses will be deducted from their liability limit, thereby reducing the liability available to settle the claim.
   c. The insured's legal expenses will be paid under the supplemental payments, but the shrinking limit provision will limit the amount available for legal expenses.
   d. The shrinking limit will have no effect on the insured's liability limit.

22. Which of the following is the best definition for the "out of state coverage extension" on an automobile policy?
   a. The limits of liability on an insured's policy is the same in all states in which they travel.
   b. The limits of liability on an insured's policy will automatically double when they travel out of state.
   c. An insured's limit of liability is not valid if they travel out of state.
   d. The insured's limit of liability will increase, if applicable, to meet the minimum liability of the state they are traveling in.

23. A business owner has a mortgage on the building where his Widget store is located, and the mortgagee is listed on their commercial property insurance policy. The business owner fails to pay his premium, and the policy is cancelled. What, if anything, is the insurance company's obligation to the mortgagee?
   a. The insurance company has no obligation to the mortgagee as the business owner is their client.
   b. The insurance company must notify the business owner in writing, advising them to tell their mortgagee that they cancelled their insurance policy.
   c. The insurance company must notify the mortgagee, in writing, of the policy cancellation.
   d. The insurance company cannot cancel the policy for unpaid premiums when there is a mortgagee listed on the policy.

24. Insurance company's use actual cash value to determine the amount of some losses. Besides replacement cost and depreciation, which other factor is sometimes used in the calculation?
   a. Broad evidence rule
   b. Repair and replace rule
   c. Valuation rule
   d. Property value determination rule

Answer Explanations

1. C: When analyzing an insurance company's risk exposure, the number of insurance companies selling policies in the state would not provide information that would assist in determining risk. Historical weather data would be useful, as weather occurrences like hurricanes and tornadoes can put the company at risk for losses. Crime reports would provide information, such as the number of burglaries and instances of vandalism, and it would help the insurance company predict losses in these areas. Highway safety tests would aid in determining vehicle-damage costs so the insurance company can charge the appropriate premium for vehicles.

2. C: Even if an insured is not present when a loss occurs, he or she could still be negligent for the loss. The third party who suffered the loss would have to prove that the insured was obligated to provide a standard of care, such as putting a fence around a hole on their property. The insured must have caused the loss, albeit unintentionally, such as by leaving a candle burning and causing a fire. The insured must have had a legal burden to prevent the loss, such as not letting an underage, unlicensed driver use their vehicle.

3. D: In order to receive insurance coverage, the insured must have an insurable interest in whatever is insured, meaning that the insured would suffer a loss in the event of a claim. The insured could purchase a property-insurance policy for property owned by the insured and their spouse, as they both have an interest in the policy. The insured could not purchase insurance for their brother's car, as the insured does not own the vehicle. Even if the insured is the beneficiary who will inherit the property upon the death of their mother, they have no insurable interest, as they do not own the home at the present time. Although the insured may work for a company, they cannot purchase insurance for the company, as they are not even part owner in the business.

4. C: Under contributory negligence, if the third party is found to be at fault for any percentage of the loss, they will receive no payment. Under comparative negligence, the insured could collect compensation, but only for the percentage of the loss that was the fault of the insured. Gross and criminal negligence do not factor into determining what party is at fault.

5. D: In the event that an insurance company discovers that an insured has provided false information, they can null and void the policy, meaning there would be no coverage for losses. They cannot require the insured to sign an affidavit, ask for proof that fines were paid, or have the insured charged criminally.

6. A: In order for a risk to be insured, the probability of loss and the attendant cost must be calculable. The insurance company needs to be able to determine what possibilities exist that a loss can occur and be able to determine the value of any losses. The premium charge, amount of profit, amount paid per loss, maximum liability limit, and number of claims are not useful in determining risk. The loss ratio is the comparison between the amount of premium collected and the number of claims.

7. A: Subrogation occurs when an insurance company pays for a loss that is found to be the fault of a third party and subsequently recoups the money they paid from the third party. Reimbursement means to pay something back. Supplemental coverage is for expenses incurred by the insurance company during the investigation, defense, and settlement of claims. Waiving the deductible is when the insurance company does not require the insured to pay a portion of a claim.

8. D: "Percentage state" is not a valid answer. File and use indicates an insurance company can file their rate change, but the state insurance board can require the rate be changed. Flex rating allows changes that are within a certain percentage. Prior approval requires the rate to be approved by the state insurance board prior to implementation.

9. B: There will be no coverage, either for property damage or bodily injury, as the insured does not own the mower; thus, the insured does not have an insurable interest. The insured cannot buy coverage for something he does not own. The other three answers are invalid.

10. A: There is no coverage if an insured is arrested for a crime and must post a bail bond to be released from jail. Claim-investigation costs, loss of earnings by the insured, and prejudgment and post judgment interest are all paid under supplemental coverage.

11. C: Property damage caused to 100 homes as the result of a tornado could cripple an insurance company financially. When this happens, insurance companies use their reinsurance policy to cover the catastrophic loss. The other three losses would not be large enough to warrant the use of a reinsurance policy.

12. A: Supplementary payments are paid by the insurance company to cover the cost of investigating, defending, and paying claims. Supplementary payments are in addition to the policy's liability limit. There can be a limit on specific supplementary payments, such as covering lost wages. Supplemental payments are not paid by the third party.

13. A: When the insured pays a deductible, they are practicing "risk retention" because they are responsible for a portion of the loss, paid as a deductible. Transference of risk occurs when one does not want to pay for the risk and delegates the responsibility to someone else, as in the insured having their risks paid for by an insurance company. Risk avoidance is taking measures to be sure the risk does not occur. Risk reduction is reducing the chances that a risk will occur.

14. A. Insurance policies are aleatory contracts, meaning the amount paid by one party is unequal to the amount paid by another party. Insured's losses often much outweigh the amount of premium they paid. Exposure is the insurance company's chance that a risk will occur. Liability, also known as casualty, is a loss suffered by a third party. Premium is the amount the insured pays for insurance.

15. C: Stock-market securities are speculative risks, as the investor could gain or lose money on the transaction. Vandalism, fire, and water damage are all pure risks because their occurrence always constitutes a loss to the insured.

16. C: While exclusions are listed under the "exclusions" section of an insurance policy, the insurance company can list exclusions anywhere in the policy wording.

17. B: Subrogation is the process by which insurance companies are reimbursed for payments they have made to cover a loss that was the fault of a third party. Valuation is the method used by an insurance company to calculate the amount of a loss. Misrepresentation is when a person gives false information or withholds pertinent information from the insurance company that would affect the risk being insured. Liberalization is when a state introduces a law that adds coverage to an insurance policy.

18. B: Since Jack purchased the underinsured motorist coverage on his personal automobile insurance policy, if Jack is in an accident where the third party is at fault, Jack's liability limit will increase to the liability limit on his policy if the third party's liability limit is lower than his. The underinsured motorist coverage only activates when the third party is at fault, and their liability limit is lower than the insured's.

19. C: Insured's are not required to get any estimates on damages as a condition of their post loss duties. They do have to take necessary action, if able to, that will prevent further loss, provide a proof of loss statement to the insurance company if requested to do so, and notify the insurance company as soon as possible after they become aware of the claim.

20. C: Pro-rata will result in the largest amount of refund from any unearned premium. Short rate will result in a lower refund. Rebate clause and penalty calculation are not valid answers.

21. B: When a liability policy has a shrinking limit provision, in the event of a claim, the insured's legal expenses will be paid from the liability limit as opposed to the supplementary payments. The insured's maximum liability limit will be reduced by the amount of their legal expenses, leaving less coverage available to settle third party claims.

22. D: When the insured is traveling in another state, if the minimum liability limit required by the state is more than the insured's liability limit, the insured's liability will automatically increase to satisfy the state's minimum liability.

23. C: In the event that a policy is cancelled, the insurance company must notify, in writing, any mortgagee listed on the policy.

24. A: The broad evidence rule will take into consideration elements such as the age and condition of the property in determining the actual cash value. The other answers are not valid.

Casualty Policy Provisions

Section II-The Casualty Section

Section II is the casualty section or liability section of a personal or commercial insurance policy. Liability insurance provides coverage for damages to third parties. The insurer is obligated to defend the insured in the event of a lawsuit, provided the loss is potentially covered under liability. For example, the insurance company would provide a defense for the insured if a third party were injured after falling down a set of stairs on an insured's property, but not if the insured were charged with breaking and entering and theft—criminal offenses.

Coverage E: Personal Liability

Personal Liability is a type of coverage that protects the insured's financial assets in the event of a lawsuit. Liability insurance was designed to provide coverage in the event a third party suffers a loss for which the insured is legally liable. An example would be if a third party is injured when he or she falls down a flight of stairs on the insured's property. When a third party suffers a loss, he or she must prove the insured was liable or negligent for his or her loss. Using the example of a third party being injured after falling down a flight of stairs on the insured's property, the third party would have to prove that it was the stairs that caused him or her to fall as opposed to simply tripping. Liability portions of an insurance policy may provide an amount of coverage that can be offered to settle a claim, regardless of who is negligent for the loss. Again, using the stair example, the insurance company may elect to pay the third party a maximum amount of $2500 to settle the claim, without having to accept liability or prove who was negligent for the loss.

Personal Liability Claims are paid on a per-occurrence or claims-made basis. A **per-occurrence basis policy** offers coverage for eligible claims as long as the loss occurred during the time the policy was in force, even if the claim is filed or reported after the policy has expired. For example, a third party sustained an injury on June 1st. The insurance policy expired on July 31st. The third party reports the claim on September 1st. As long as the third party can establish his or her loss occurred on June 1st—when the insurance policy was in force—coverage may be in place even though the third party reported the claim after the policy expired.

A **claims-made basis policy** offers coverage for eligible claims only if the loss occurred during the policy period and if the loss is reported before the policy expires. In the above example, even though the loss occurred during the policy period, there would not be coverage as it was reported after the policy expired. An insured may be able to purchase **extended coverage**—also known as a **tail**—for policies issued on a claims-made basis if the insured continues, without interruption, to renew the policy with the same insurance company. In this instance, again using the above example, coverage for the loss to the third party may be available if the insured renewed the policy with the same company when it expired on July 31st, and the insured had purchased extended coverage.

Coverage F: Medical Payments

Medical payments cover third party losses regardless of who was at fault for the loss. Examples of medical payments include ambulance fees, emergency room fees for services and diagnostic testing, and funeral expenses, as long as the loss was a result of a peril covered under the liability portion of the policy. Amounts paid to cover third party medical payments are deducted from the aggregate limit on the policy. The **aggregate limit** is the most an insurance company will pay for all damages incurred by a third party. For example, if the policy aggregate limit was $1,000,000, and the insurance company paid $10,000 to cover medical payments incurred by a third party, there would be $990,000 left to cover any further damages awarded to the third party.

Coverage E and F exclusions

The following exclusions apply to all liability policies:

- Acts by the insured that are expected or intentional
- Acts related to business
- Portions of a dwelling that are rented and not used as a residence
- War or acts of war—whether or not war is declared
- Communicable diseases that are transmitted by the insured
- Physical or mental abuse, including corporal punishment and sexual molestation
- Use, sale, or possession of controlled substances, except for the legal use of prescription drugs
- Possession, use, maintenance, loading, or unloading of watercraft, aircraft, and motor vehicles

Coverage E does not apply to property that the insured uses, owns, or maintains. Personal liability does not cover cost of loss assessments that are required by a homeowner or property owners' association or any corporation where the insured is a member. Coverage E does not cover liability that is covered under other contracts when the loss occurred away from the insured location or when the contract covered the liability of others before the incident occurred. Homeowner policies exclude losses for liability that are covered by Nuclear Energy Liability policies.

Coverage F excludes losses for injuries sustained by resident employees when they are not related to the employee's duties for the insured and are not sustained at the insured's location. Medical payments will not cover bodily injuries that are caused by nuclear reactions or exposure to radiation or contamination. Coverage F excludes coverage for losses involving organized or competitive auto or motorcycle racing.

Liability Specifics

Liability, as it pertains to commercial general, automobile, and property insurance, contains particulars specific to those policies.

When coverage is provided for a claim, the insured will usually be required to pay a portion of the loss, known as the **deductible**. Policies can contain different deductible amounts depending on the type of claim that is filed. For example, an insured may have a deductible of $250 for collision claims and a deductible of $100 for comprehensive claims on an auto policy. Companies may waive the deductible, meaning it does not have to be paid by the insured, if the claim is over a certain amount. Companies may also lower the deductible, sometimes eliminating it entirely, for every year the insured goes without a claim. There are no industry standard rules that must be followed by all insurance companies in relation to deductibles. Each insurance company has the liberty to waive and/or reduce deductibles and set specific deductibles for various losses.

Supplementary Payments for Coverages A & B

As stated previously, supplementary payments are allotted to cover expenses incurred in the process of investigating, defending, and settling a claim. There can be limitations on the amount of the expenditures. For example, an insured's lost wages may be limited to $250 per day.

Indemnitee (Third Party) Defense Costs

If an indemnitee (third party) sustains a loss covered by the insurance policy (an insured peril), the defense costs will be paid from the limit stated on the policy. For example, if the liability limit is $1,000,000, the indemnitee's defense costs will be deducted from the $1,000,000. However, if the insured and the indemnitee are both named in a lawsuit, the indemnitee's defense costs will be paid as a supplementary payment, provided the liability is covered by the insured' s policy.

Policy Conditions

When the insured becomes aware of a situation that could result in a liability claim by a third party, even in the absence of a claim being filed, the insured is responsible to do the following:

- Promptly notify the insurance company of the claim, or advise the insurance company of a potential claim and provide details pertaining to the loss.
- Cooperate with the insurer to the best of their ability during the process of investigating, defending, and settling the claim.
- Forward any documents to the insurance company they have or receive concerning the claim (e.g., correspondence from a lawyer or notices from the court).
- Maintain written notes related to the claim, such as the circumstances surrounding the loss, and provide the notes, if requested, to the insurer. Insurance companies rely heavily on the insured's accurate record keeping when handling claims.
- Assist the insurance company with procuring information, when requested (e.g., providing the insurance company with a copy of the lease agreement to which the insured is a party).
- Facilitate communication with persons who are libel to the insured.
- With the exception of rendering first-aid treatment during or immediately following an incident, the insured must not make any promises or agreements with third parties, unless given permission to do so by the insurer. For example, the insured cannot advise a third party that the insurance company will cover the cost of their medical bills without having that directive come from the insurance company.

Insurance Policy Nonrenewal Requirement

If the insurance company is not going to offer **renewal** of a commercial general insurance policy, they must notify the insured in writing no less than thirty days before the expiry date. Known as the "**when we do not renew condition**," this only applies to the insurance company. The insured may choose not to renew the policy when it expires simply by not paying the premium.

Valuation Condition

When determining the amount payable in the event of a loss, the **valuation condition** defines how the amount of coverage will be calculated and reimbursed. The following guidelines are used when calculating coverage amounts.

- When payment is being made for restitution due to a property loss, the insurance company will pay the lesser of the cost to repair the property, the cost to replace the property, or the limit of the insurance policy. For example, if paying for the loss of a building and the cost to repair the damage is $10,000, the cost to replace the building is $50,000, and the insurance limit is $100,000, the insurance company would choose to repair the damage.

- When payment is to cover a securities loss, the insurance company will use the face value of the securities at the close of business on the day the loss occurred. For example, if the value of the securities lost was $25,000 at the close of business on the day the loss occurred, the insurance company would cover only $25,000 no matter how much the value of the securities may have fluctuated between the time of the loss and when restitution is paid to the insured.

- When money is being covered, the insurance company will pay the face value of the money.

Limit of Liability and Supplementary Payments - Personal Auto Policy

Limit of Liability - Part A - Personal Auto Policy

Stated in **Part A** of a personal auto policy is the policy limit. The policy limit is the maximum amount of coverage provided to cover damage suffered by a third party when the insured is found to be responsible for the damage. Note that supplementary payments are separate from the policy limit and do not affect the maximum amount of coverage provided. The policy can state the maximum third-party liability limit in two ways: a single limit or a split limit. If stated as a single limit, then all third-party losses are paid from that amount. For example, if the single limit is $100,000, the policy would cover damages up to that amount. Split-limit coverages differ in that there are maximums allotted for specific types of losses. When stated as a split limit, three consecutive numbers, separated by a slash (/), are used to indicate the amount of coverage available for each type of loss. For example, if the split limit is reflected as 25/60/15, the coverage would be limited to $25,000 for bodily injury sustained per person, $60,000 for bodily injury sustained per occurrence, and $15,000 for property damage sustained per occurrence.

Supplementary Payments - Part A - Personal Auto Policy

As stated previously, **supplementary payments** are allotted to cover expenses incurred in the process of investigating, defending, and settling a claim, and there can be limitations on the amount of the expenditures.

Liability Exclusions - Part A - Personal Auto Policy

- Damage to property owned or being transported by the insured (For example, there is no coverage if the insured is moving their piano on a trailer, and the piano is damaged.)
- Damage to property the insured is renting, borrowing, or has care of
- Bodily injury to an employee of the insured
- Damage that occurs while a vehicle owned by the insured is being operated as a public or livery conveyance, except when operated as a share-the-expense carpool (For example, there is no liability coverage if the insured is operating their vehicle as a taxi.)
- Damage incurred while the insured is using their vehicle in any kind of auto business
- Any damage arising from the insured possessing or operating a vehicle that they do not have permission to use or possess
- Damage that is caused intentionally by the insured
- Any loss that is otherwise covered by a nuclear-energy liability policy
- Damage caused by any vehicle that has less than four wheels or is designed specifically for use off of main roads (e.g., an all-terrain vehicle)
- Losses incurred that involve a vehicle owned by the insured that is not listed on their insurance policy
- Damage arising from the use of a vehicle that is not covered but is used or owned by family members
- Damage incurred while practicing for or participating in any prearranged racing or speed contest

Liability Exclusions - Part B - Personal Auto Policy

- Damage caused as the result of operating a vehicle with less than four wheels or a vehicle not designed for use on main roads
- Losses incurred while the insured's vehicle was being used as a public or livery conveyance, except in the case of a share-the-expense carpool
- Losses sustained while using or occupying any vehicle used as a residence or premises
- Any damage that is intentionally caused by the insured
- Losses occurring as a result of being employed when workers' compensation benefits are required or available to cover bodily-injury claims
- Losses as a result of using, or being struck by, a vehicle (other than those covered on the insured's policy) that is owned by or furnished for the use of the insured
- Losses as a result of using, or being struck by, a vehicle that is not insured but is owned or used regularly by a family member of the insured

- Losses caused by occupying a vehicle being used for business purposes
- Losses as the result of the insured operating a vehicle they do not have permission to use or have a reasonable expectation they would be entitled to use
- Losses caused by a vehicle that is not insured, even if the insured owns the vehicle
- Losses as a result of preparing for or participating in any prearranged racing or speed contest
- Losses resulting as a consequence of war (either declared or undeclared), civil war, insurrection, rebellion, revolution, terrorism, or discharge of a nuclear weapon (even if accidental)

Liability Exclusions - Part C - Uninsured Motorist - Personal Auto Policy

- Damage as the result of the insured driving a vehicle they own but not listed on their personal auto policy
- Damage arising from a loss when the vehicle involved is being used as a public or livery conveyance, except when the vehicle is being used as a share-the-expense carpool
- Damage incurred when the vehicle is being used in the operation of a business
- When coverage for any damage is being paid for by another means, such as workers' compensation, as that would constitute duplication of coverage
- If someone other than the insurance company offers or guarantees payment without the permission of the insurance company
- Losses as the result of the insured operating a vehicle they do not have permission to use
- Bodily injury sustained by the insured's family member when they are in an automobile owned by the insured but covered under another policy

Umbrella Liability Policy

Umbrella liability policies provide additional liability coverage over and above the maximum amount of insurance declared on the insured's personal auto, personal property, and boat policies. As with all policies, umbrella liability policies have exclusions:

- Damage to property owned by the insured
- Losses related to any business practices
- Intentional damage caused by the insured
- Damage as a result of contracts entered into by the insured (For example, an electrician hired by the insured sues the insured.)
- Any malpractice lawsuits
- Claims otherwise covered by another entity, such as workers' compensation
- Any losses caused by the insured as a result of criminal activity

Practice Questions

1. Third-party losses are covered under what section of an insurance policy?
    a. Endorsements
    b. Casualty
    c. Exclusions
    d. Riders

2. An insured has one vehicle insured on a personal auto policy. They use the vehicle as a taxi, but only on weekends. One Saturday afternoon, the insured accidentally rear-ends a third party. Will the insured's personal auto policy cover the damage to the third party?
    a. Yes, but only the damage to the third party's vehicle
    b. No, business use is excluded from coverage
    c. Yes, but only for damage to the insured's own vehicle
    d. Yes, because the vehicle was only used as a taxi part time

3. Which of the following is NOT true about deductibles?
    a. Insurance policies can have more than one deductible.
    b. Deductibles can be waived by the insurance company.
    c. Deductibles are a form of risk retention.
    d. The third party must pay the deductible before settling a claim.

4. Which of the following does the insured NOT do when they are made aware of a potential claim?
    a. Forward any documents concerning the claim to the insurance company
    b. Assist the insurance company when gathering information pertaining to the claim
    c. Notify the insurance company of a potential claim
    d. Advise the third party that their damages will be covered by the insurance company

5. An insured rents a room in an owner-occupied home to a non-family member. The insured drains the pool but neglects to tell their renter. The renter runs into the backyard, does a cannon ball into the empty pool, and is injured. How will the insured's property policy deal with the bodily-injury claim?
    a. The insurance company will pay the bodily-injury claim and subrogate against the insured.
    b. The insurance company will not pay more than the maximum policy limit.
    c. The insurance company will only cover the bodily injury if the pool was properly fenced.
    d. The insurance company will offer no coverage for the bodily-injury claim.

6. Purchasing an umbrella policy will provide what benefit to the insured?
    a. Liability coverage for intentional acts by the insured
    b. Additional workers' compensation coverage
    c. Additional liability coverage
    d. Coverage for catastrophic losses

7. Defining how coverage will be calculated and reimbursed is known at what condition?
    a. Valuation
    b. Replacement
    c. Restitution
    d. Loss

8. The maximum liability limit of $100,000 stated as a split limit, 20/40/40, covers which of the following?
   a. $20,000 maximum for bodily injury per person, $40,000 maximum total for property damage, $40,000 maximum payout per claim
   b. $20,000 maximum for bodily injury per person, $40,000 maximum for bodily injury per occurrence, $40.000 maximum property damage per occurrence
   c. $20,000 maximum total for property damage, $40,000 maximum for bodily injury, $40,000 maximum for bodily injury and property damage combined
   d. $20,000 maximum for supplemental payments, $40,000 maximum for bodily injury to the insured, $40,000 maximum for property damage to the insured

9. Insurance was founded on what basic principle?
   a. Determining liability
   b. Developing a formula to calculate premiums
   c. Spreading risk
   d. Providing coverage for all losses

10. Which of the following is a requirement of the "when we do not renew condition" in regard to renewal of a commercial liability policy?
   a. The insured must pay the renewal in full.
   b. The insurance company must give the insured fifteen days to find coverage elsewhere.
   c. The insured must notify the insurance company no more than thirty days after renewal is offered.
   d. The insurance company must notify the insured in writing no less than thirty days before expiry.

Answer Explanations

1. B: Third-party losses are covered under the casualty section of an insurance policy. Endorsements are additions to insurance policies that amend clauses stated in the policy. Exclusions are perils that are not covered in an insurance policy. Riders are similar to endorsements in that they amend the coverage stated in the insurance policy.

2. B: If a vehicle listed on a private auto policy is engaged in any kind of business, coverage for any and all losses will be denied. Therefore, the damage to the third party's vehicle, damage to the insured's vehicle, and any bodily injury caused while the vehicle was being used in a business, including as a taxi, is not covered.

3. D: Under the casualty coverage on an insurance policy, there are no deductibles. In the event of a loss, the insured could be responsible to pay a deductible. Insurance policies often have more than one deductible that will be applied in the event of a loss. For example, on an auto policy, the collision deductible could be $500, and the comprehensive deductible could be $250. Insurance companies often waive deductibles depending on the loss. Deductibles are a form of risk retention as the insured is often responsible to pay a portion of all losses.

4. D: The insured must never tell a third party that their loss will be covered by their insurance. This directive has to come directly from the insurance company. The insured is required to forward documents pertaining to the claim to their insurance company, assist the insurance company in gathering necessary information, and notify their insurance company if they become aware that the potential exists for a claim.

5. D: No coverage will be available for bodily injury as the third-party lives with the insured. The other three answers are not valid responses.

6. C: Umbrella policies provide additional liability, or casualty, coverage for an insured. Liability is never covered for intentional acts of the insured. Workers' compensation is an insurance policy on its own for which no additional coverage is available, as it would constitute dual coverage. Coverage for a catastrophic loss, if it is an insured peril, would usually be paid from the insurance company's reinsurance policy.

7. A: Valuation defines which calculations will be used when the insurance company is paying a loss. Replacement is a coverage option in the case of a loss. Paying someone back for something they lost is restitution, but it is not explicitly an insurance term. A loss is the opposite of a gain.

8. B: When listed as a split limit, there are three numbers separated by slashes (/). The first number indicates the amount of coverage for bodily injury per person. The second number indicates the amount of coverage for bodily injury per occurrence. The third number indicates the amount of coverage for property damage per occurrence. Insurance policies universally use this split-limit detail.

9. C: Insurance was founded on the principle of spreading risk, whereby premiums paid for by many will cover losses suffered by only a few. Determining liability and developing a formula to calculate premiums are insurance processes. No insurance policy will provide coverage for all losses.

10. D: In order to satisfy the "when we do not renew condition," if the insurance company is not going to renew a commercial liability policy, they must notify the insured, in writing, no less than thirty days before the current policy expires. The other three answers are not valid.

Dear Property and Casualty Test Taker,

We would like to start by thanking you for purchasing this study guide for your exam. We hope that we exceeded your expectations.

Our goal in creating this study guide was to cover all of the topics that you will see on the test. We also strove to make our practice questions as similar as possible to what you will encounter on test day. With that being said, if you found something that you feel was not up to your standards, please send us an email and let us know.

We would also like to let you know about other books in our catalog that may interest you.

SIE Study Guide

This can be found on Amazon: amazon.com/dp/1628459328

Series 7 Study Guide

amazon.com/dp/1628458976

We have study guides in a wide variety of fields. If the one you are looking for isn't listed above, then try searching for it on Amazon or send us an email.

Thanks Again and Happy Testing!
Product Development Team
info@studyguideteam.com

Interested in buying more than 10 copies of our product? Contact us about bulk discounts:
bulkorders@studyguideteam.com

FREE Test Taking Tips DVD Offer

To help us better serve you, we have developed a Test Taking Tips DVD that we would like to give you for FREE. **This DVD covers world-class test taking tips that you can use to be even more successful when you are taking your test.**

All that we ask is that you email us your feedback about your study guide. Please let us know what you thought about it – whether that is good, bad or indifferent.

To get your **FREE Test Taking Tips DVD**, email freedvd@studyguideteam.com with "FREE DVD" in the subject line and the following information in the body of the email:

a. The title of your study guide.

b. Your product rating on a scale of 1-5, with 5 being the highest rating.

c. Your feedback about the study guide. What did you think of it?

d. Your full name and shipping address to send your free DVD.

If you have any questions or concerns, please don't hesitate to contact us at freedvd@studyguideteam.com.

Thanks again!

Made in the USA
Monee, IL
25 August 2024

64544227R00092